Pieced
or Appliquéd
FLOWERS

From the AQS Contest
FLOWERS ON PARADE

American Quilter's Society
P. O. Box 3290 • Paducah, KY 42002-3290

Located in Paducah, Kentucky, the American Quilter's Society (AQS) is dedicated to promoting the accomplishments of today's quilters. Through its publications and events, AQS strives to honor today's quiltmakers and their work and to inspire future creativity and innovation in quiltmaking.

EDITOR: BARBARA SMITH

BOOK DESIGN/ILLUSTRATIONS: JARRETT SIMS AND ELAINE WILSON

COVER DESIGN: MICHAEL BUCKINGHAM

PHOTOGRAPHY: CHARLES R. LYNCH

Library of Congress Cataloging-in-Publication Data

Pieced or Appliquéd Flowers: From the AQS Contest Flowers on Parade /
Edited by Barbara Smith
p.cm.
ISBN 1-579432-742-9
1. Patchwork--Patterns. 2. Quilting--Patterns. 3. Appliqué--Patterns.
4. Flowers in art
I. Smith, Barbara (Barbara F.) II. American Quilter's Society.

TT835 .P545 2000
746.46'041--dc21   00-038995
                                                    CIP

Additional copies of this book may be ordered from the American Quilter's Society, PO Box 3290, Paducah, KY 42002-3290 @ $18.95.

Dedication

This book is dedicated to all quilters who have ever entered a contest. Your willingness to show your work to others, to test your skills in competition, to learn by doing, inspires us all.

Acknowledgments

The American Quilter's Society would like to thank the quilters who entered the Flowers on Parade Contest. It was challenging to choose the winners because the quilts were all so beautiful.

Contents

The Contest 6

How to Use This Book 7

Parade of Quilts 8

THE WEDDING QUILT by Alice Dunsdon 10

ROSEBUD by Patricia Gabriel 28

COCKSCOMB by Martha Plager 36

A BOUQUET FROM MY QUILTING FRIENDS by Reggie Gross . .46

TRY TO REMEMBER by Dawn Cameron-Dick 54

DAYLILIES by Janis Benedict 64

HOFFMAN HYBRID LILY by Chris Taricani 72

Special Techniques

3-D Rosebuds 49, 57

3-D Hexagons 33

Bias Tubes .57

Brick Border 50

Extra-Wide Binding 15

Quick-Pieced Flying Geese 75

Yo-yo Flowers 33

The Contest

The Design-A-Quilt Contest: Flowers on Parade was sponsored by the American Quilter's Society. For the contest, quilters were invited to submit wall or bed quilt designs to be published in this pattern book, and the focus was traditional or traditional-with-a-twist quilts.

The entries were judged by American Quilter's Society staff members. Selection of winners was based on beauty, originality, and construction.

How to Use This Book

The quilts are the original creations of the makers and represent various quiltmaking techniques. They vary in difficulty of construction, but all require at least basic sewing and quiltmaking skills. This book is not designed to teach those skills, but it does include instructions for some of the methods used. (See the Special Techniques section on the Contents page.)

It is always difficult to assess the skill level required for making a particular quilt. Many beginning quilters who are comfortable with sewing and who are patient can tackle a quilt pattern that would baffle a much more experienced quilter. To make the patterns accessible to more quilters, each contains information on how to simplify construction. These suggestions may also be helpful for a more experienced quilter who wants a faster project.

Included with each pattern is an introduction to the quiltmaker and the story of how she designed her quilt. It is our hope that the quiltmakers and the quilts will inspire you to try your hand at designing.

The pattern instructions include full-size patterns for making templates and cutting fabric patches, and measurements for those pieces that can be easily rotary cut.

Parade of Quilts

PIECED OR APPLIQUÉD FLOWERS

TRY TO REMEMBER,
Dawn Cameron-Dick, pg. 54

THE WEDDING QUILT,
Alice Dunsdon, pg. 10

DAYLILIES,
Janis Benedict, pg. 64

HOFFMAN HYBRID LILY,
Chris Taricani, pg. 72

COCKSCOMB,
Martha M. Plager, pg. 36

A BOUQUET FROM MY QUILTING FRIENDS
Reggie Gross, pg. 46

ROSEBUD
Patricia Gabriel, pg. 28

PIECED OR APPLIQUÉD FLOWERS

Meet Alice Dunsdon

My mother introduced me to quilting when she offered me a top she had pieced in the early 1920s. Her challenge to me was, "If you quilt this, you can have it." I knew nothing about quilting, but having sewn my own clothing for over 30 years, I thought, "What's so tough about this? Boring, to be sure, but it's do-able."

I dug in my heels and began a struggle that nearly defeated me. "So what," I said. "It's my first quilt...and it will be my last!" Surprise! By the time the quilt was done, I was hooked. Boring? Hardly. Instead, there is contentment, peacefulness, fulfillment, catharsis...but never boredom. In the 20 years since, I have made approximately 100 quilts.

I have given some lectures and taught quilting. Some of my quilts have won honors in national and international shows, while others have appeared in national magazines and *The New York Times*. However, my proudest accomplishment was teaching my two granddaughters, Rebecca and Sarah, to quilt, starting them when they were just 13 and 14 years old.

My husband of 47 years, Don, and I live on our farm in southwest Iowa, where I have the opportunity to garden when I'm not quilting. Our two children and five grandchildren live nearby.

Designing THE WEDDING QUILT

This quilt was created for an AQS contest. Having missed the deadline by eight days, I entered it in a Good Housekeeping/Land's End Contest instead. It was juried into the top 250 quilts out of 4,500 entries. The fabrics in the quilt had been given to me as part of a prize package from yet another quilt that had been entered in a different contest.

In the past, I had used the traditional method to make a Double Wedding Ring quilt, and its difficulty had so rankled me that I was determined there had to be an easier way. THE WEDDING QUILT was drawn full-size on a piece of freezer paper by using two cake plates for patterns. The six rings overlap around a nosegay of flowers appliquéd in the center – a bride's bouquet?

Because I use a design-as-you-go method, I transferred the pattern to cloth. The design was good, but it seemed to need some more bridesmaid's bouquets, thus my inspiration for the border design.

I drew one-fourth of the border design on freezer paper and added a few more circles with plates. When satisfied with the drawing, I traced it on cloth, arranged the four corner sections on a larger than needed white background, and placed the bride's bouquet in the center. The open spaces between the designs in the border were then closed with leaves and circles for a good line flow.

I had conquered the double wedding ring, and the different sizes of rings had given it a more exciting look. I only hope that they never stop making freezer paper!

THE WEDDING QUILT, 50" x 50", made by Alice Dunsdon

The Wedding Quilt
Pattern

Freezer-paper foundations make the sewing of the arcs much easier than traditional piecing methods. The challenge in making this quilt is in the appliquéing of the overlapping pink and white background fabrics, described on page 15.

To simplify this project, use one background fabric 52" x 52" (2 panels 26½" x 52", 3 yds.) in place of the pink and white fabrics listed in the yardage table. Appliqué the rings, leaves, flowers, and circles directly to the background.

Buying and Cutting

Fabrics	Yds.	No. of Pieces
Pink	3¼	center square 22"
		4 squares 20"
		4 border strips
		12¾" x 50½"
Pink scraps	1	ring sections
Pink to red scraps	¾	flowers, circles
Green	⅜	1 square 12"
Green scraps	⅓	leaves
White	1¼	1 square 39"
Backing	3¼	2 panels 25½" x 54"
Binding	⅞	6 strips 4½" wide
Batting		54" x 54"

Paper Foundation Templates
(without seam allowances)

Arcs	4 #1, 8 #2, 8 #6, 8 #8, 8 #9, 6 #10
Tails	8 #4, 8 #4r, 4 #7, 4 #7r, 6 #11, 6 #11r

Note: r = reverse. Arc and tail foundations will be easier to handle if they are made from sturdier paper than freezer paper.

Freezer-Paper Templates
(without seam allowances)

Flowers	5 A, 14 B, 2 D, 2 F, 11 G, 1 H, 36 J
Leaves	73 K
Circles	13 C, 12 E, 12 L, 9 M, 2 N, 64 P, 27 R, 9 S, 4 T, 4 W
Intersections	4 #3, 4 #3r, 8 #5, 8 #5r, 6 #12
Quilt center	1 hexagon
Placement	6 center
	1 border Y
	1 border Z
	1 border Zr

Arc Construction

1. Make the number of paper foundations listed in the table for arcs and tails, and make freezer-paper templates for the intersections. Full-sized patterns begin on page 17. Be sure to label all of the pieces carefully.

2. Use the flip-and-sew method of paper piecing to sew the arcs and tails. When all the foundations have been covered, trim the allowances to ³⁄₁₆".

3. Turn under and baste the allowances on the two long sides of each arc and tail section, leaving the two ends unturned. When working on the inner curve of the arcs, you will need to clip the fabric at intervals. Figure 1 shows a basted piece from the back side.

Center Ring Construction

1. You are now ready to sew the six arcs (Section 10) to the 22" square of pink fabric. To find the center of this square, fold it in half both ways and gently press the folds. With the square right side up, arrange the center placement templates, shiny side down, as shown in Figure 2. Press the templates to the fabric.

2. Position all six center arcs and the 12 tails (Section 11) and baste them in place. Remove the templates. Appliqué along the inside of each arc.

3. To prepare the intersections, press the six freezer paper templates (Section 12) on the wrong side of the fabric. Cut out the patches, leaving a ³⁄₁₆" turn-under allowance. Turn the allowance under and baste. Baste the tails and intersections in place (Figure 3).

4. Turn to the back side. Trim away the background under the arcs to within ¼" of the appliqué stitching, as shown in Figure 4, page 14.

5. Turn the center ring piece right side up. Center it on the 39" white square, also right side up. Pin and

Unturned end

Unturned end

Fig. 1. Back side of basted ring section.

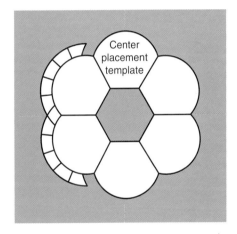

Center placement template

Fig. 2. Centered templates with two arc sections in place.

Fig. 3. Appliqué stitches shown in red; basting, green.

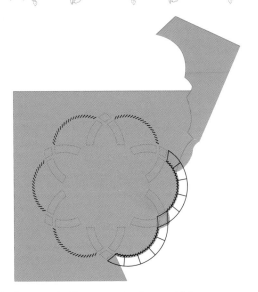

Fig. 4. Wrong side. Trim away background fabric.

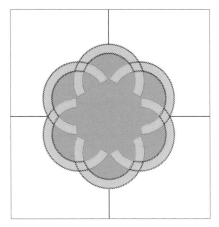

Fig. 5. Appliqué outside edges of arcs to the white background. Appliqué stitches shown in red; basting, green.

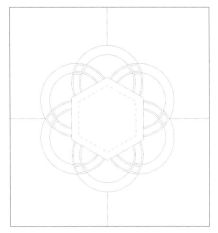

Fig. 6. Sew the hexagon over the center.

baste. Appliqué the outside edges of the arcs to the white background. Appliqué the intersections. Do not appliqué the tails yet (Figure 5).

6. Turn to the back side and trim the white background away from behind the appliqué to within ¼" of the stitching. Be careful not to cut through to the front. Remove the paper templates from behind the arcs and intersections.

7. Make the rest of the templates. Use the hexagon template (page 18) to cut a green piece of fabric. With right sides facing up, position the green hexagon over the center so that it overlaps the raw ends of the tails. There is no need to turn under the raw edge of the hexagon because the appliqué flowers will cover it. Securely sew the piece in place ½" in from the edges all around (Figure 6). On the back, trim away the fabric from behind the hexagon to within ¼" of the stitching.

8. For the flowers, leaves, and circles, press freezer paper templates to the wrong sides of the appropriate fabrics. Cut the fabric pieces out, leaving a ³⁄₁₆" turn-under allowance. Turn and baste the allowances.

9. Arrange the flowers, leaves, and circles on the center ring section. The placement need not be exact, but make sure that all the raw edges of the hexagon are covered. Baste and then appliqué these pieces and the tails. Remove all the basting and trim away excess fabric from behind the flowers, leaves, and tails. Remove the paper templates from behind the flowers and tails.

Border Ring Construction

1. Sew the pink border strips to the quilt and miter the corners (Figure 7). Set aside.

2. On the right side of one of the pink 20" squares, press placement templates Y, Z, and Zr, shiny side down as shown in Figure 8.

PIECED OR APPLIQUÉD FLOWERS - Alice Dunsdon

3. Snug fabric arc sections 1, 2 and 9 against the templates and baste them in place. Remove the templates and add the intersections and tails by using what has already been basted as a guide.

4. Appliqué the inside edges of the arcs, the long edges of the tails, and the intersections, as shown in Figure 9. The outside edges of the arcs will be appliquéd to the pink border. Remove the basting stitches.

5. Leaving a ¼" allowance, trim the pink fabric away from under arc sections 1, 2, and 9, as shown in Figure 10 (see page 16). Leave the rest of the pink square untrimmed for now. Repeat steps 2–5 to make three more border ring pieces for the corners of the quilt.

6. Place the border ring pieces in the corners of the quilt, centering them on the mitered seams. Baste, then appliqué the outer edges of arc sections 1, 2, and 9 (Figure 11, see page 16).

7. Position, baste, and appliqué the flowers, leaves, and circles to the border, trimming away the rest of the pink fabric as you appliqué. Add two leaves (K) and three circles (C, T, and W) at the center of each side to cover the border seam.

Quilting Pattern

THE WEDDING QUILT is quilted in grid patterns punctuated with quilted rings.

Extra-Wide Binding

1. Cut 45° angles on each end of the binding strips. Join the strips end-to-end with a ¼" seam allowance. Press the seam allowances open. Fold the strip in half lengthwise, right side out. Press.

2. Start pinning the binding to the quilt near the center of one side. Position the binding parallel to the

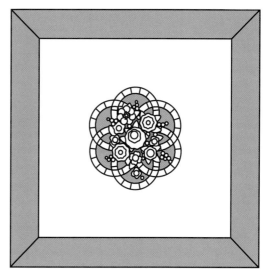

Fig. 7. Sew pink border strips to the quilt and miter the corners.

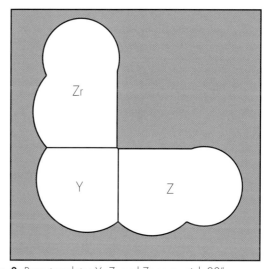

Fig. 8. Press templates Y, Z, and Zr on a pink 20" square.

Fig. 9. Appliqué the arc edges shown in red.

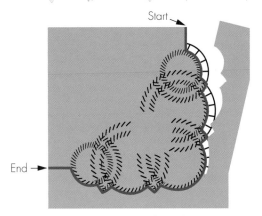

Fig. 10. Wrong side. Trim the pink fabric from under arc sections 1, 2, and 9 only.

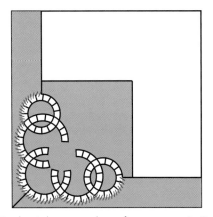

Fig. 11. Appliqué the outer edges of arc sections 1, 2, and 9 to the pink border.

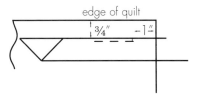

Fig. 12. Place binding ¾" from the edge.

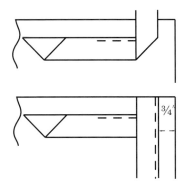

Fig. 13. Fold binding upward, then straight down.

edge of the quilt, but ¾" away from its edge (Figure 12). Raw edges of binding should be facing outward.

3. When beginning to sew, plan on leaving at least a 6" tail of binding for ease in pinning and sewing later. Stitch ¼" in from the raw edges of the binding. This stitching will be 1" from the quilt edge.

4. Stitch to within 1" of the first corner. Backstitch. Cut the threads and remove the quilt from the machine.

5. Fold the binding strip diagonally upward, then fold it straight down, leaving the folded edge flush with the top edge of the quilt. The binding strip will lie ¾" away from the edge of the quilt (Figure 13).

6. Stitch ¼" from edge of binding. Handle all corners in this way. When you're back to where you started, stop sewing within 6" of that point.

7. Bring the two ends of the binding together and trim any excess. Join the ends with a diagonal seam. Complete by stitching the remaining binding to the quilt.

8. You may want to trim excess fabric from the corners to eliminate bulk. Fold the binding over the raw edge of the quilt to the back side. Slip-stitch in place, mitering each corner as you come to it.

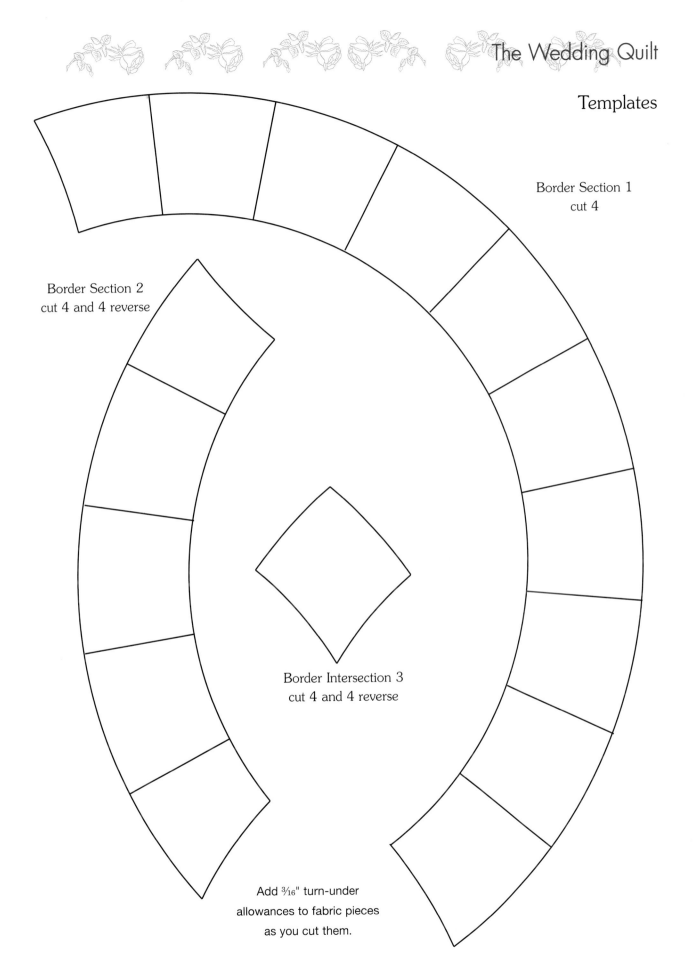

Border Section 1
cut 4

Border Section 2
cut 4 and 4 reverse

Border Intersection 3
cut 4 and 4 reverse

Add ³⁄₁₆" turn-under
allowances to fabric pieces
as you cut them.

Templates

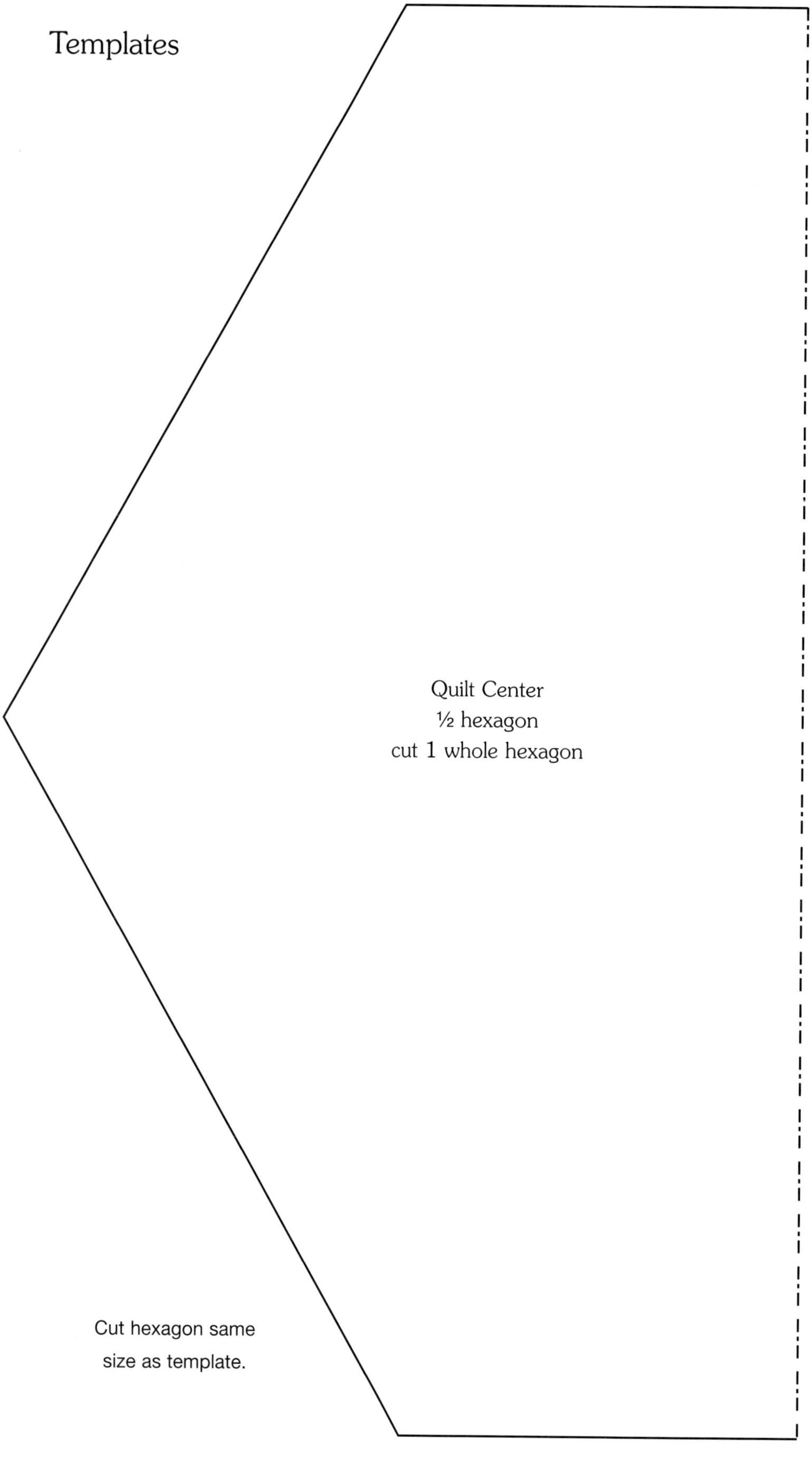

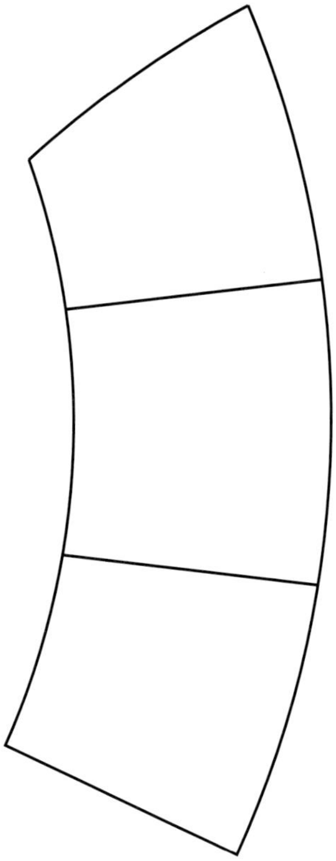

Quilt Center
½ hexagon
cut 1 whole hexagon

Border Tail Section 4
cut 8 and 8 reverse

Cut hexagon same
size as template.

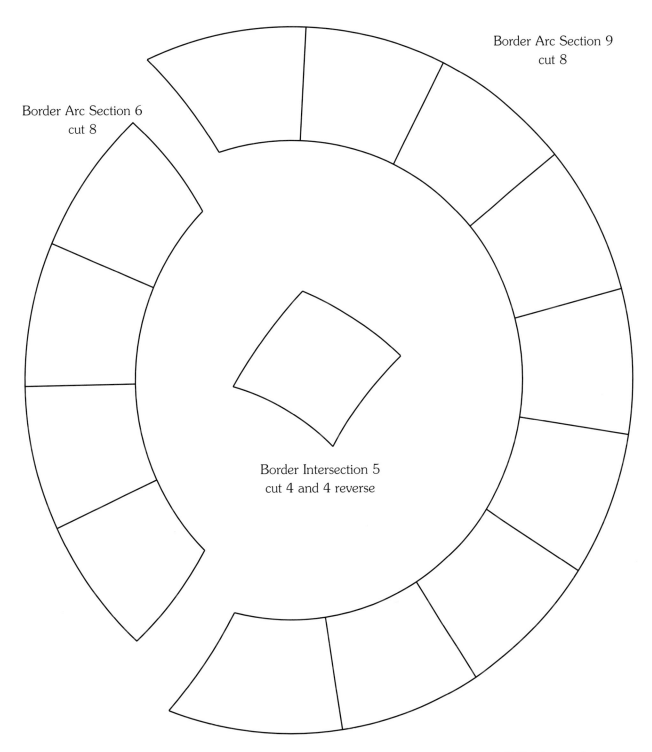

Border Arc Section 9
cut 8

Border Arc Section 6
cut 8

Border Intersection 5
cut 4 and 4 reverse

Add ³⁄₁₆" turn-under
allowances to fabric pieces
as you cut them.

Templates

Add ³⁄₁₆" turn-under
allowances to fabric pieces
as you cut them.

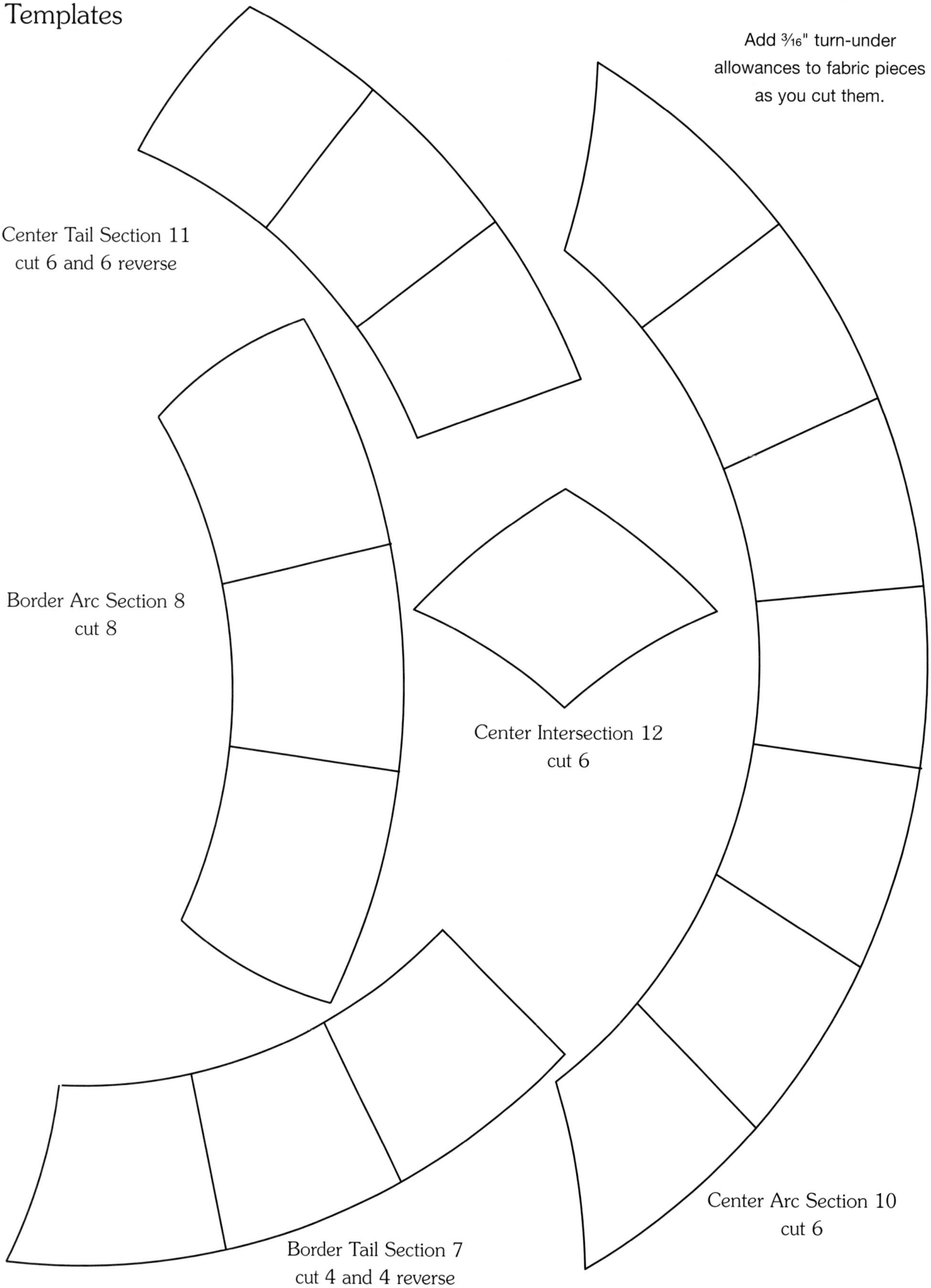

Center Tail Section 11
cut 6 and 6 reverse

Border Arc Section 8
cut 8

Center Intersection 12
cut 6

Center Arc Section 10
cut 6

Border Tail Section 7
cut 4 and 4 reverse

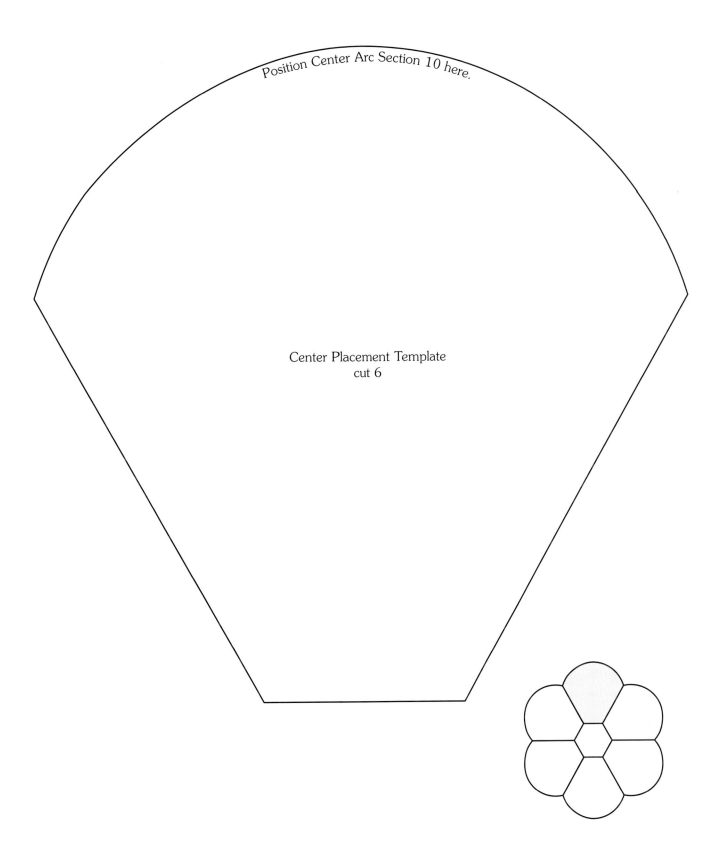

Position Center Arc Section 10 here.

Center Placement Template
cut 6

Templates

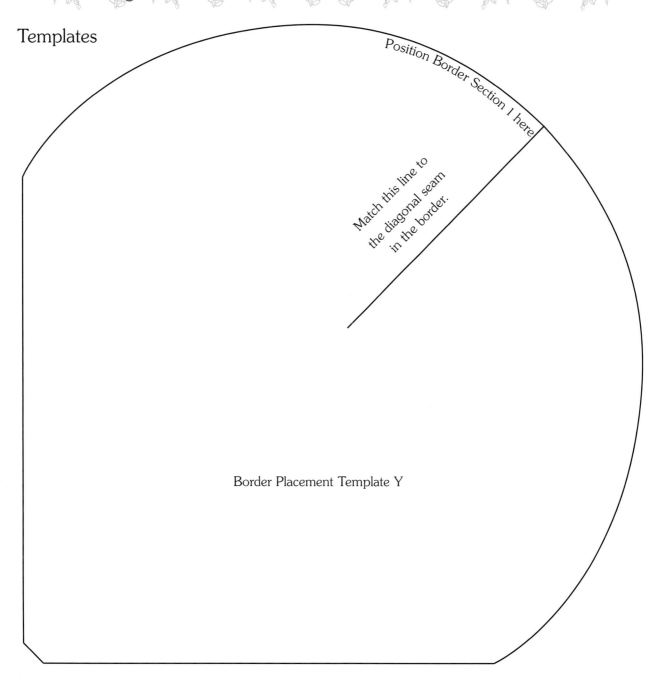

Position Border Section 1 here

Match this line to the diagonal seam in the border.

Border Placement Template Y

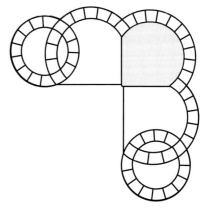

PIECED OR APPLIQUÉD FLOWERS - Alice Dunsdon

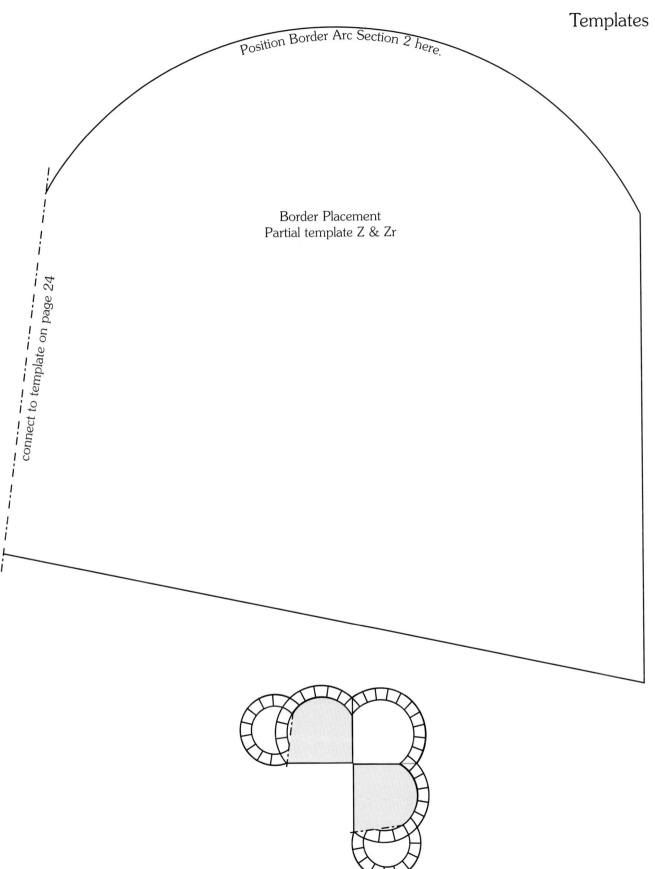

Position Border Arc Section 2 here.

Border Placement
Partial template Z & Zr

connect to template on page 24

Templates

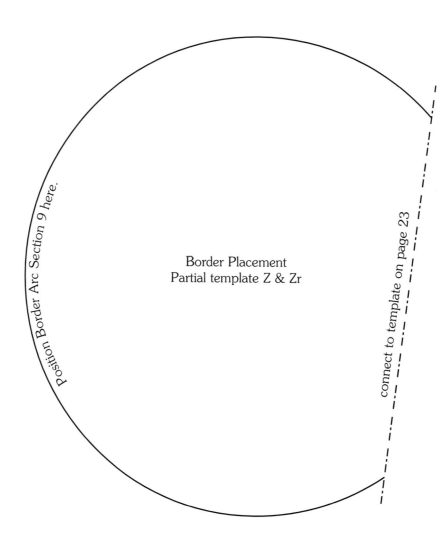

Position Border Arc Section 9 here.

Border Placement
Partial template Z & Zr

connect to template on page 23

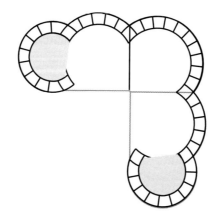

PIECED OR APPLIQUÉD FLOWERS - Alice Dunsdon

Templates

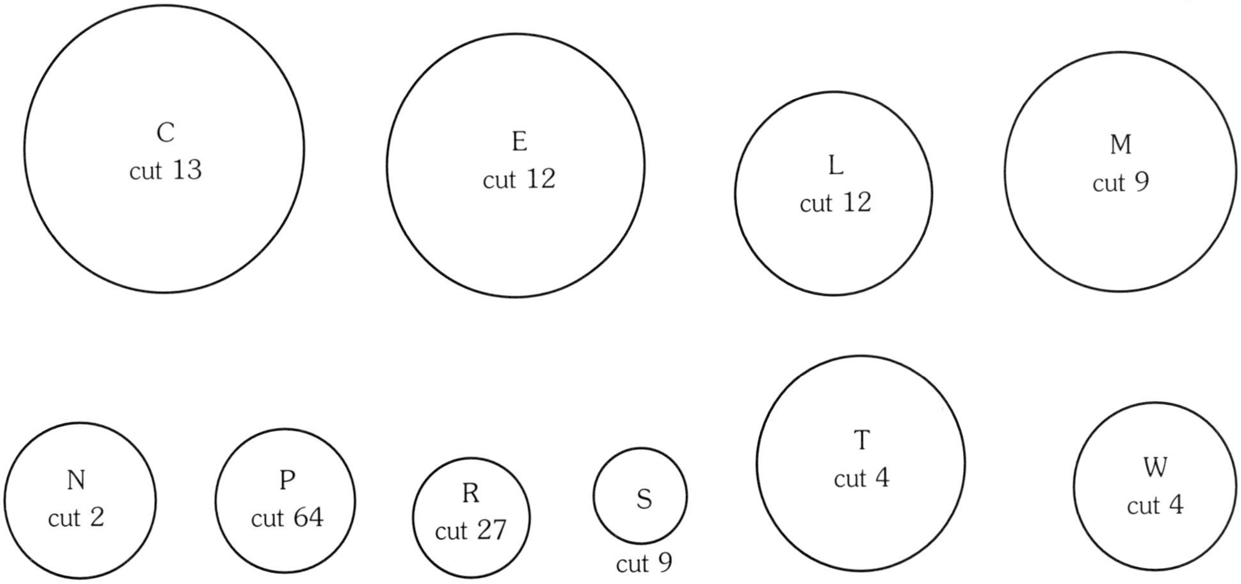
C
cut 13
E
cut 12
L
cut 12
M
cut 9
N
cut 2
P
cut 64
R
cut 27
S
cut 9
T
cut 4
W
cut 4

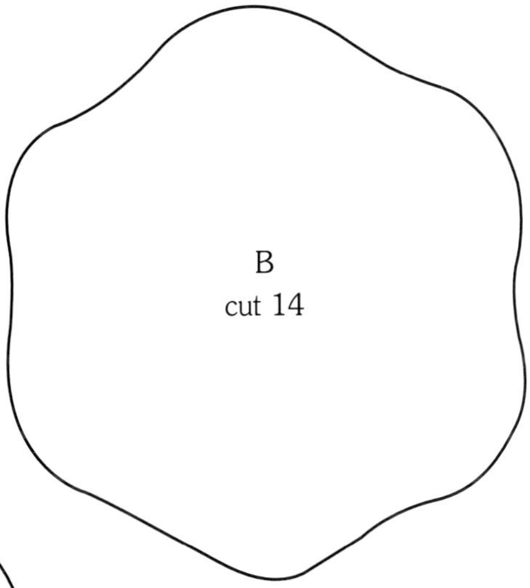
B
cut 14

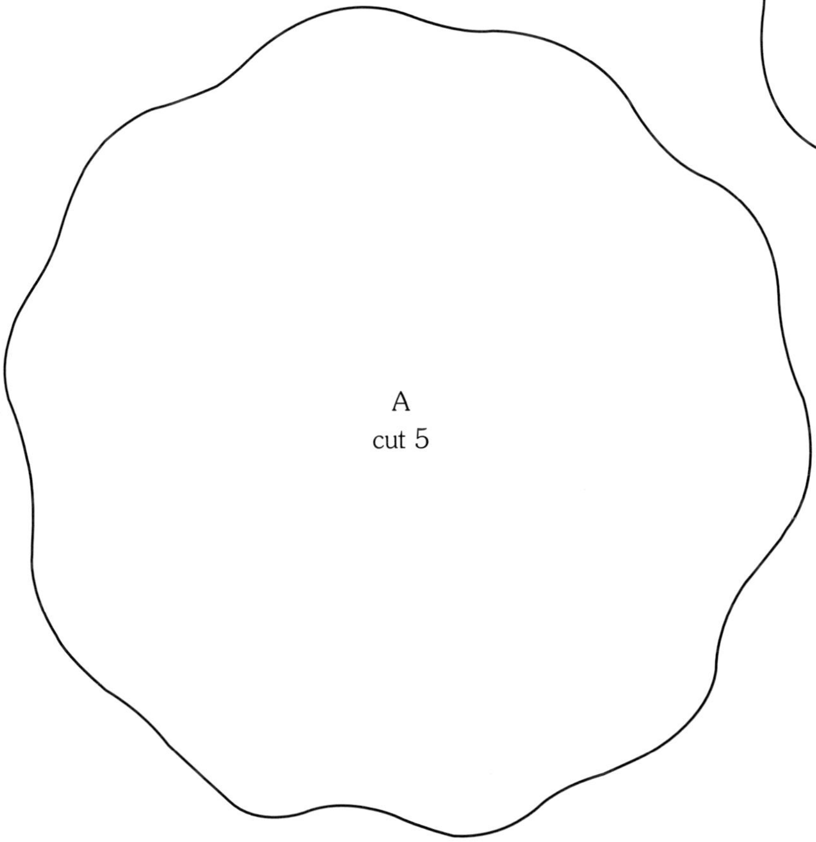
A
cut 5

Add $\frac{3}{16}$" turn-under allowances to fabric pieces by eye as you cut them.

Templates

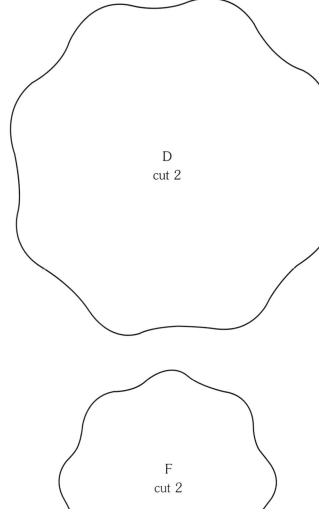

D
cut 2

H
cut 1

F
cut 2

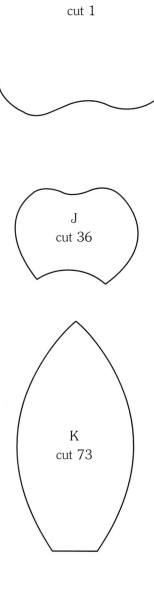

J
cut 36

K
cut 73

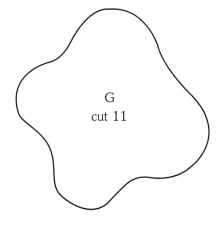

G
cut 11

Add 3/16" turn-under
allowances to fabric pieces,
by eye, as you cut them.

PIECED OR APPLIQUÉD FLOWERS - Alice Dunsdon

Border Appliqué Placement

Place flowers and leaves as desired
to make a pleasing arrangement
and to cover ends of tail sections.

Center Appliqué Placement

Meet Patricia Gabriel

Entering a new millennium with 10 years of devotion to the art of quiltmaking, I find myself meeting new challenges every day. My quilting style is generally described as scrap-method, and my quilt designs are based on personal interpretation of traditional patterns.

Originally, I hand quilted everything, and now, after endless hours of practice, machine quilting feels comfortable to me. I make quilts for competition and publication, and they later become gifts for family and friends.

I feel fortunate in having the ability to enjoy all aspects of quiltmaking from design to finish. While design gives my quilts form and motion, color is what brings them to life and makes them sing. I always have several quilts in progress at any given time so that, whether I'm designing, cutting, sewing, or quilting, the variety of options allows me to focus energy where I find the most satisfaction and excitement.

Designing ROSEBUD

ROSEBUD was designed as a result of redecorating a guest room in my home. I had the option of using either a traditional headboard for the king-sized bed or a quilt that would give the illusion of a headboard. I decided to make a personal statement with an original design.

Soft moss green was selected for the carpeting and walls, and the duvet, dust ruffle, and window treatments contained pink roses and stripes of green, white, and a touch of yellow. The quilt is made from soft, restful hues of this palette. I affectionately dubbed the redecorated room "The Rose Room" after hanging a picture of tea roses painted by my husband, Richard. Fittingly, the quilt is named for our daughter, Rosemary, whose nickname is Rosebud.

ROSEBUD, 57" x 84", made by Patricia Gabriel

Rosebud
Pattern

The quilt is constructed in a series of "border" rows with all the blocks set on point, making it much easier to put together than it might appear. So, if you are an experienced sewer who has made at least a couple of quilts, you will enjoy making this beauty.

For best effect, choose a wide range of values from two different color families. The fabrics in the quilt range from the palest rose to the deepest burgundy and from pastel green to deep green.

To simplify this project, you can omit the more time-consuming Grandmother's Flower Garden and Appliqué blocks. Use the remaining blocks to make a smaller quilt or make more of the easier blocks to use as substitutes.

Buying and Cutting

Fabrics	Yds.	No. of Pieces
Rose scraps	3	193 A, 104 B, 40 C, 24 E, 24 F, 14 G, 28 J, 96 K, 16 M
Green scraps	1½	80 A, 86 B, 56 F, 16 N, 16 P
Floral scraps		4 L
White scraps	1⅞	76 A, 6 B, 24 E, 28 G, 28 H, 4 L, 16 K
hexagon blocks		16 squares 6½"
White	2	120 A, 160 B, 40 C 40 D
side triangles		7 squares 9¾"
corner triangles		2 squares 9⅜"
Backing	5¼	2 panels 32½" x 89"
Binding	¾	8 strips 2" wide
Batting		64" x 89"

Freezer-paper foundations
(without seam allowances)
Grandmother's Flower Garden blocks
112 hexagons

Templates
Appliqué blocks
1 each of three sizes of circles

Supplies
Green embroidery thread for appliqué blocks
Thread for basket handles

Block Construction

Make the following numbers of blocks, following the block diagrams for assembly, the Buying and Cutting chart for number of patches, and the quilt photo for color placement.

16 Pastel Nine-Patch blocks: Make these blocks with soft pastel colors and white, five pastel and four white squares for each block.

20 Darker Nine-Patch blocks: Make these with four light and five dark squares.

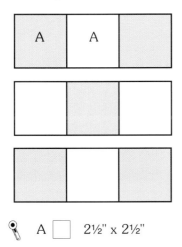

A ☐ 2½" x 2½"

Nine-Patch block assembly

3 Nine-Patch blocks with corner triangles: These three blocks are used in the center of the quilt.

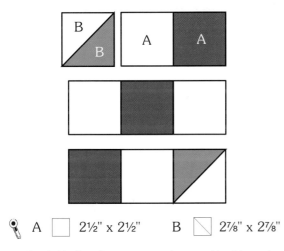

A ☐ 2½" x 2½"   B ◸ 2⅞" x 2⅞"

Nine-Patch block with corner triangle assembly. Note placement of darker squares in corners.

40 Rosebud blocks: This block is constructed like a Nine Patch. Be careful that the leaves are pointing in the right direction.

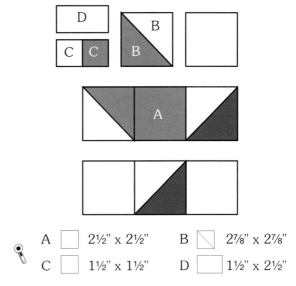

A ☐ 2½" x 2½"   B ◸ 2⅞" x 2⅞"
C ☐ 1½" x 1½"   D ☐ 1½" x 2½"

Rosebud block assembly

16 Grandmother's Flower Garden blocks: Use English paper piecing to construct the hexagons for the blocks, as follows:

Press the hexagon freezer-paper foundations to the wrong side of the fabric. Cut out the patches, leaving a ¼" seam allowance by eye around each one. Turn the seam allowances to the back and baste. Join hexagons by hand with tiny overcast stitches, or by machine with a zigzag stitch. Remove the basting stitches and the papers.

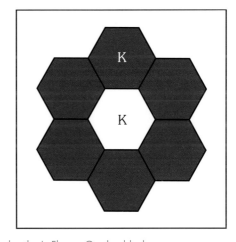

Grandmother's Flower Garden block

After assembling the posies, appliqué them to the 6½" background squares. Turn the blocks over and trim away the background behind the appliqué.

6 Pinwheel blocks: Simple pinwheel blocks in pastel shades are framed Log Cabin-style. Use the following partial-seam method to sew the frames: Sew the first frame strip (F patch) to the block, leaving about ½" unsewn on the right end, as shown in Figure 1. Add subsequent frame strips counterclockwise (Figure 2). After adding the last strip, finish sewing the seam of the first strip.

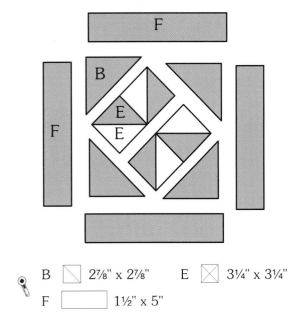

| B | | 2⅞" x 2⅞" | E | | 3¼" x 3¼" |
| F | | 1½" x 5" | | | |

Pinwheel Block assembly. Make six yo-yos from 1½" circles, page 34, and place one in the center of each block.

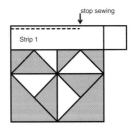

Fig. 1. Leave at least ½" unsewn.

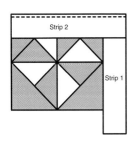

Fig. 2. Working counterclockwise, add second strip.

4 Floral-Fabric blocks: The frames of the 4½" floral fabric squares are set off by corner squares.

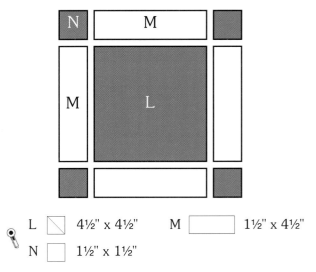

| L | | 4½" x 4½" | M | | 1½" x 4½" |
| N | | 1½" x 1½" | | | |

Floral-Fabric Block assembly

14 Basket blocks: These simple basket blocks are framed the same way as the Pinwheel Blocks. Use two strands of embroidery thread, perle cotton, or couched cord to make the basket handles.

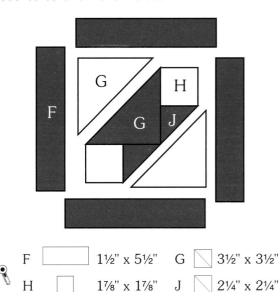

| F | | 1½" x 5½" | G | | 3½" x 3½" |
| H | | 1⅞" x 1⅞" | J | | 2¼" x 2¼" |

Basket Block Assembly

4 Appliqué blocks:

3-D hexagons – Use the circle templates for the 3-D hexagon (page 34) to cut out four circles. Fold each circle in half twice to find the center. Mark the center on the wrong side of the fabric with a pencil dot. Fold one edge to the dot and finger press the

fold. Moving around the circle, fold the edge to the center again and press (Figure 3). Continue folding until a hexagon has been formed (Figure 4).

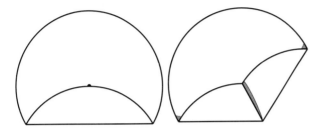

Fig. 3. Fold edge to dot; then fold second edge to dot.

Fig. 4. Finished hexagon.

Yo-yos – Cut 12 circles for appliqué yo-yos (page 34). Turn under a ¼" allowance around each circle. Sew the allowances to the circles with a running stitch and pull the threads to gather the circles (Figure 5).

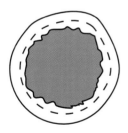

Fig. 5. Sew turn-under allowance with a running stitch and pull thread to gather.

Scalloped yo-yos – Scallop the edges of four of the yo-yos by sewing through the center from top to bottom and back to the top. Then go around the outside and come up from the bottom in the center. Pull the thread tight. Repeat these steps three times to form the four petals (Figure 6).

Fig. 6. Pull edges in with thread to form "petals."

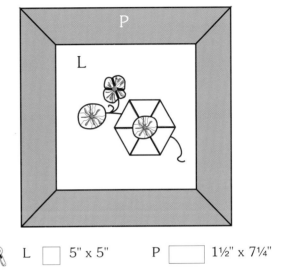

| | L | ☐ | 5" x 5" | P | ☐ | 1½" x 7¼" |

Appliqué block assembly. Trim L to 4½" x 4½" after appliquéing. Add P rectangles and miter the corners.

Quilt Assembly

After all the blocks have been made, arrange them on a flat surface, paying close attention to orientation. You may want to play with them to see if there is another assembly that appeals to you. It is helpful to use a sticker to label every block within each diagonal row (Fig. 7).

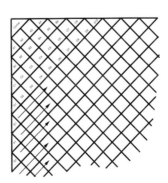

Fig. 7. Labeling the blocks by diagonal rows will help avoid confusion as you sew the blocks together.

To make the four corner triangles, cut the two 9⅜" squares in half diagonally. Cut the seven 9¾" squares on both diagonals to make the side triangles. Add these triangles to your layout.

Sew the quilt together in diagonal rows, including the side triangles, then sew all the rows together. Sew the corner triangles last.

Sew the two backing panels together lengthwise. Layer the backing, batting, and quilt top, and baste the layers together.

Quilting Pattern

Because of the complexity of the pieced design, the quilting has been kept simple. Outline and straight-line quilting predominate.

Finishing

Use your favorite method to bind the quilt. There are enough 2" strips to make double-fold binding with mitered corners. One of the little framed squares might make a good background for a label.

Templates

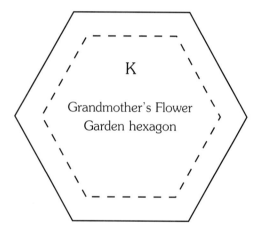

K

Grandmother's Flower
Garden hexagon

Circle for Appliqué
Block yo-yos

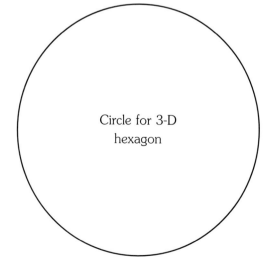

Circle for 3-D
hexagon

Circle for
Pinwheel yo-yo

Rosebud - Pattern Layout

Meet Martha Plager

Ever since my first home-economics class in ninth grade, I have been in love with fabric and garment sewing. Quiltmaking is not in my family background, but when we moved to Louisville, Kentucky, in December 1988, I met several people who quilted. My first quilting class was in March 1989. By the time my first 24" wallhanging was complete, I was hooked on this new passion.

The first quilt show I ever attended was the 1989 American Quilter's Society show in Paducah, Kentucky, when Caryl Bryer Fallert won Best of Show with her CORONA OF THE SUN. This is still a favorite quilt of mine. Many years later, I find myself just as enthusiastic about quiltmaking as in the beginning. One can never have too many quilts, and quilting is a wonderful way to play with fabric. I actually don't visit the fabric stores as often as I did as a garment sewer. Quilting takes more time, and I don't need to acquire fabric quite so regularly. Although, if you saw my fabric closet, you might wonder about this statement.

Although I love to machine piece my quilts, hand quilting is soothing and relaxing. I am always quilting when watching TV with my husband, going to meetings, or traveling long distance. My friends know me as a person who has a project to accomplish but wants to talk to you while doing it.

Designing COCKSCOMB

This original design was inspired by the first cockscomb that grew in my garden, in the summer of 1998. I had been a vegetable gardener for many years and was just starting to experiment with flowers. A trip to France and Monet's garden at Giverny inspired me to put some energy into growing flowers as well as quiltmaking.

I just loved the intense fuchsia color of the blossoms and the variety of shapes, which would make an interesting quilt. I need to feel emotionally involved in my subject to be enthusiastic about a project, and it is fun to develop an idea into a design and then to make the design a reality in a quilt.

During the designing of COCKSCOMB, I could just imagine using my luscious hand-dyed fabric. To give the blossoms more texture, commercial fabrics, such as the check, were used as well.

To design the piece, I drew several blossom shapes on paper, made tracing-paper copies of them, and then simply arranged them on blank paper of the general size needed for the quilt. Altering the size of some of the same blossom shapes made the piece more interesting. For me, drawing is a difficult task, so I try to make it simple by breaking the process down into easy steps.

COCKSCOMB, 37" X 48", made by Martha Plager

Cockscomb
Pattern

This quilt is entirely machine pieced. The background has been cut into sections to facilitate construction. To make the flowers, you can string piece them on paper foundations (see Quilt Construction, page 39); make your own fabric by strip or crazy piecing, then cut out the flowers; or cut the flowers whole from a suitable fabric.

To simplify this project, appliqué the flowers, stems, and leaves to a background fabric.

Buying and Cutting

Fabrics	Yds.	No. of Pieces
Red scraps	¾	7 flowers, pieced
Green scraps	¾	7 stems 29 leaves
Background Border	1½ 1⅜	pieced 2 strips 4" x 43½" 2 strips 4" x 39½"
Backing	1⅝	1 panel 41" x 52"
Binding	½	5 strips 2½" wide
Batting		41" x 52"

Supplies

Freezer paper – 30" x 41" piece
Tracing paper
Carbon paper
Ultra-fine permanent markers, black and red

Quilt Construction

1. Trace the flower patterns (pages 41-45) on tracing paper. Cut out the flowers and arrange them on the 30" x 41" piece of freezer paper, shiny side up.

2. Use a black ultra-fine permanent marker to trace the patterns on the shiny side of the freezer paper. Add stems and leaves, as desired, free-hand. In the background areas, draw seam lines as needed to simplify the sewing of the flowers (Figure 1). This tracing will be cut into templates for cutting fabric pieces.

3. Using carbon paper, make another copy of the whole design on tracing paper to use as a master pattern reference during the construction of the quilt.

4. On the freezer-paper drawing, use a red ultra-fine permanent marker to make tic marks along the seam lines and to mark V's at the seam intersections to aid in matching pieces (Figure 2).

5. Place a piece of carbon paper under the freezer-paper drawing and retrace the tic marks and intersection marks. Now, you will be able to see these marks after you have ironed the patterns to the wrong side of the fabric. Cut the freezer-paper templates apart.

6. To string-piece the flowers, sew strips of various widths to the freezer-paper foundations. After the foundations have been filled, trim away the excess fabric, leaving a ¼" seam allowance by eye.

7. Use the rest of the freezer-paper templates to cut out the leaves, stems, and background fabric pieces, again eyeballing a ¼" seam allowance around

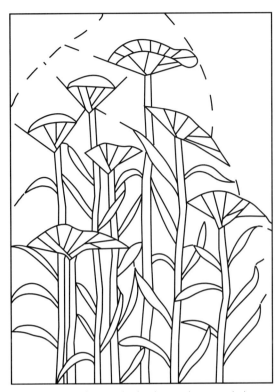

Fig. 1. Draw seam lines in the background, as needed.

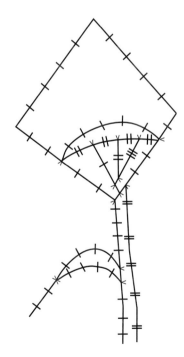

Fig. 2. Use tic marks on seam lines and V's at seam intersections to help as you match fabric pieces.

each one. Mark all the tic and intersection marks on the fabrics.

8. Arrange all the pieces on a flat surface. Sew them together in logical units, then sew the units together. Return the sewn sections to the layout each time to help you keep track.

9. Sew the 43½" border strips to the sides of the quilt, and trim the ends even with the quilt edges. Sew the 39½" strips to the top and bottom of the quilt and trim as before.

10. Layer the backing, batting, and quilt top. Baste the layers together.

Quilting Pattern

Martha has quilted along the lines suggested by the patterns in the background and border fabrics, and she has quilted down the center of some of the leaves and flower fabrics. See the detail photos below.

Finishing

Use your favorite method to bind the quilt. There are enough 2½" strips to make continuous double-fold binding with mitered corners. Note that a red accent has been added to the binding on the top and bottom of the quilt.

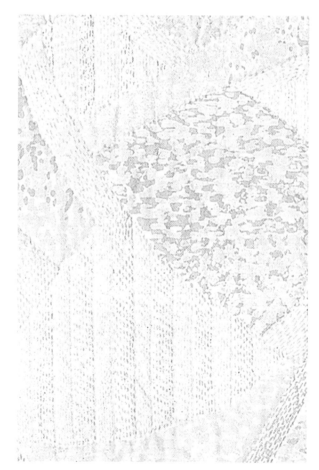

Flower Templates

Add ¼" seam
allowance to all fabric
pieces when cutting.

Flower Templates

Add ¼" seam allowance to all fabric pieces when cutting.

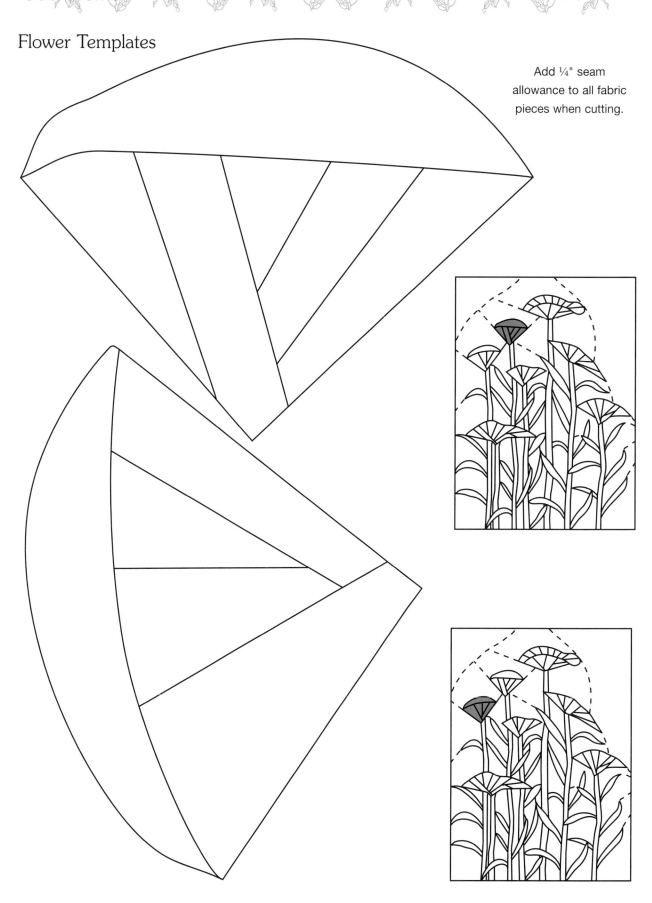

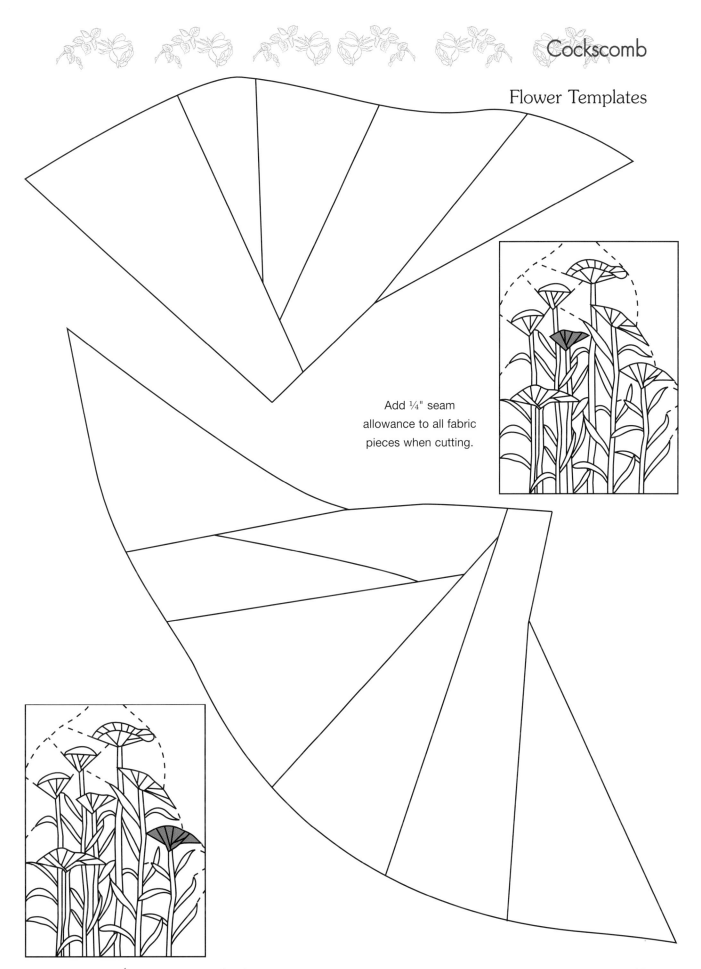

Add ¼" seam allowance to all fabric pieces when cutting.

Flower Templates

Add ¼" seam
allowance to all fabric
pieces when cutting.

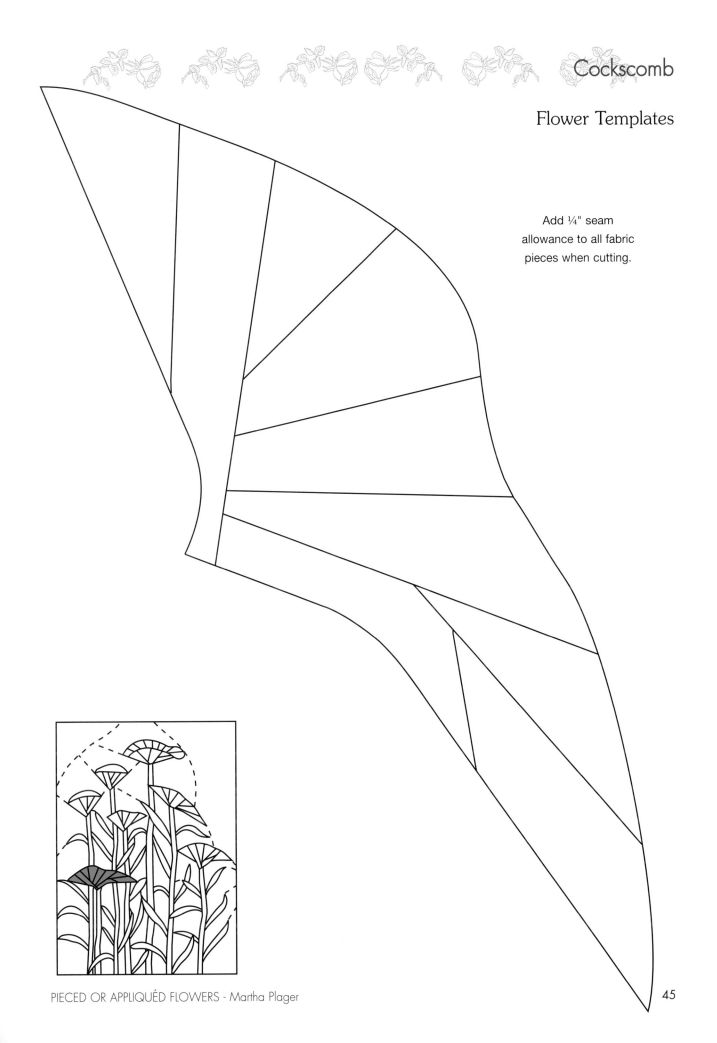

Flower Templates

Add ¼" seam allowance to all fabric pieces when cutting.

PIECED OR APPLIQUÉD FLOWERS - Martha Plager

Meet Reggie Gross

As a mother of five and the daughter of a quilter, sewing has always been an important part of my life. But I didn't begin to quilt seriously until the grandbabies started to arrive. Then I got busy making baby quilts. That's what grandmas do.

When my husband, Ed, and I retired, we wanted to leave our cold Michigan winters, so we moved to Arizona in 1990, and there my quilting life began. Here in Sun City, my friends come from all over the country. They are the most talented and devoted quilters, who are happy to share their ideas, experience, and knowledge. They are my support group.

I am a slow hand quilter and seem to do my best when working alone. I enjoy appliqué, machine piecing, and fabric manipulation. My excitement and joy as a quilter come from creating something different, trying a new idea, and seeing it to completion.

I don't seem to do well in quilt classes. Everyone is always ahead of me and working faster and better. But the teachers somehow seem to get their messages across, and I come away an improved and recharged quilter.

Guess I'm just a little grandmother sitting here enjoying her quilting as my mother did and hoping generations to come will find this same pleasure.

Designing A BOUQUET FROM MY QUILTING FRIENDS

Just a little history behind this friendship quilt – about five years ago, I belonged to a chapter of the Arizona Quilting Guild called A to Z Quilters. Just for fun, 12 members started a block exchange. Lucky quilter Number One chose her pattern, a house in any style or color. She received 11 different house blocks. Quilter Number Two wanted any star pattern in red and white. Number Three wanted Dresden Plate designs in pastels, and so on. I was the last, Number 12.

I chose the traditional Grandmother's Fan, which has always been one of my favorite quilt patterns. Because the quilt design needed uniformity, I supplied the fan pattern, drawn on 12" freezer-paper squares, and the material, which was available in many colors. Thus, my flower quilt was born.

Ten three-dimensional butterflies on the back of the quilt contain the name and color of the squares made by each guild member. My Friendship Quilt will always be very precious and special to me. It is truly A BOUQUET FROM MY QUILTING FRIENDS.

A BOUQUET FROM MY QUILTING FRIENDS, 90" x 120", made by Reggie Gross

A Bouquet From My Quilting Friends
Pattern

This delightful quilt contains 13 Grandmother's Fan blocks in several colorways of the same fabric. These 13 blocks are set with 29 plain squares. However, Reggie's quilt contains 13 all navy blue fans in place of some of the plain squares to give added texture. She has also quilted the fan pattern in five of the plain squares. The quilt is machine pieced and hand quilted.

To simplify this project, replace the butterfly fan blocks and use plain blocks for the background instead of the navy blue fans. Outline quilt the flowers and grid quilt the background.

Templates
(without seam allowances)

Fan blade
2 leaves
Flower center
Bud 1
Bud 2
small butterfly wing with body
Large butterfly wing with body, 2 pieces

Supplies
Navy and yellow embroidery thread for butterflies

Buying and Cutting

Fabrics	Yds.	No. of Pieces
Light blue	7/8	16 blades
		2 rectangles 7½"x12½"
		2 rectangles 7" x 8½"
Medium blue	5/8	16 blades
Light rose	1⅛	20 blades
bias tube		1 square 15"
Medium rose	7/8	20 blades
		2 buds (4 pieces)
Light purple	3/4	12 blades
		wing parts
bias tube		1 square 15"
Medium purple	5/8	12 blades
		2 buds (4 pieces)
		wing parts
Pink	7/8	8 blades
		2 buds (4 pieces)
		wing parts
bias tube		1 square 15
Yellow	½	8 flower centers
		(quarter circles)
		2 butterfly bodies
Green	1¾	7 large leaves
		8 small leaves
		5 flower centers
		(quarter circles)
		9 buds (18 pieces)
bias tube		1 square 28"
border accent		8 strips 1" x 42"
*Navy	6½	42 squares 12½"
border		2 strips 3½" x 92½"
		2 strips 3½" x 104½"
binding		11 strips 2½" x 42"
Leftovers		
border bricks		2½" strips, random
		lengths
Backing	8¼	3 panels 36" x 94"
Batting (gray)		94" x 106"

*To replace 13 background squares with fan blocks, buy another 1½ yards of navy.

Templates

Make templates for the pieces listed in the table. Use the templates to cut out fabric patches, adding allowances to the pieces, by eye, as you cut. Make the number of patches listed in the Buying and Cutting chart.

Fan Blocks

1. Arrange the fan blades for the flowers. Sew the blades together in groups of eight to make each block.

2. Appliqué the 13 fans to 12½" navy background squares, then appliqué the flower centers (Figure 1). Carefully trim away the background fabric from behind the appliqué.

3. Arrange all the blocks and plain squares on a flat surface in seven rows of six blocks each. Sew the blocks together in rows, then sew the rows together.

Appliqué

Bias tubes – Make 14 yards of green bias tubing from the 28" square, and two yards of the other two colors from the 15" squares, as follows: Cut continuous bias strips 1¼" wide. Fold strips in half lengthwise, right side out. Sew tubes with a ¼" seam allowance. Trim allowance to ⅛". Use a bias bar to press the seam to the back so it will not show.

Buds – Notice that there are two different three-dimensional buds. Cut two pieces of fabric for each bud.

Sew the two pieces, right sides together, leaving the bottom open. Turn the buds right side out and fold the bottom seam allowances to the inside.

For Bud 1 (pattern, page 53), add a little stuffing, if desired. Lay the appropriate bias stem on the bud and fold the stem end under to hide the raw edge.

Fig. 1. Grandmother's Fan

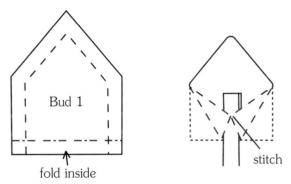

Fig. 2. Fold bud around bias stem. Full-sized pattern on page 53.

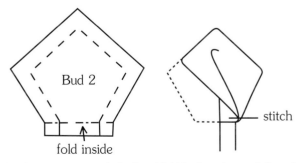

Fig. 3. Insert stem inside bud and fold bud as shown. Full-sized pattern on page 53.

Tack in place with a couple of stitches where they won't be seen. Fold the bottom corners of the bud to the center and stitch them together, as shown in Figure 2 (see page 49).

For Bud 2 (pattern, page 53), insert the raw stem end inside the bud so it doesn't show. Fold the bud as shown in Figure 3 (see page 49) and stitch.

Butterflies – Trace a butterfly wing on each light blue rectangle, including placement lines for internal wing parts. Appliqué the wing parts on the blue rectangles, then cut the butterfly wings, leaving a ³⁄₁₆" turn-under allowance. Appliqué the bodies first, then the wings.

Appliqué – Arrange the bias tubes, butterflies, and leaves on the quilt and appliqué them in place.

Borders

Brick border – From the leftovers of every fabric, cut 2½"-wide strips into bricks of varying lengths for the border. Sew the bricks together, end to end, in random order, to create the lengths needed for the border strips. Create four borders in this manner and apply each one separately, sewing first the sides and then the top and bottom.

Outer border – Sew the green border accent strips to the navy blue border strips. Then sew the borders to the quilt and miter the corners.

Quilting Pattern

Layer the backing, batting, and quilt top; baste. Use the fan pattern to create a quilting pattern for hand quilting. The flowers are echo-quilted, and swirls similar to those formed by the bias tubes are included along with some leaf patterns.

Finishing

Use your favorite method to bind the quilt. There are enough 2½" strips to make continuous double-fold binding with mitered corners.

Templates

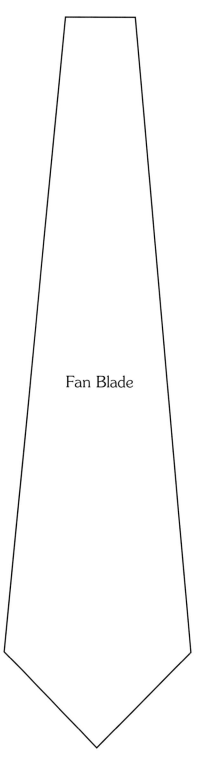

Fan Blade

Add ¼" seam allowances by eye when cutting fabric pieces.

Small Butterfly Right Wing. Reverse pattern for left wing. Add ³⁄₁₆" turn-under allowances to each piece. Shaded lines indicate embroidery.

Add ¼" seam allowances to flower center by eye when cutting fabric pieces.

Flower Center

Templates

Add ¼" seam allowances by eye when cutting small and large leaf patches.

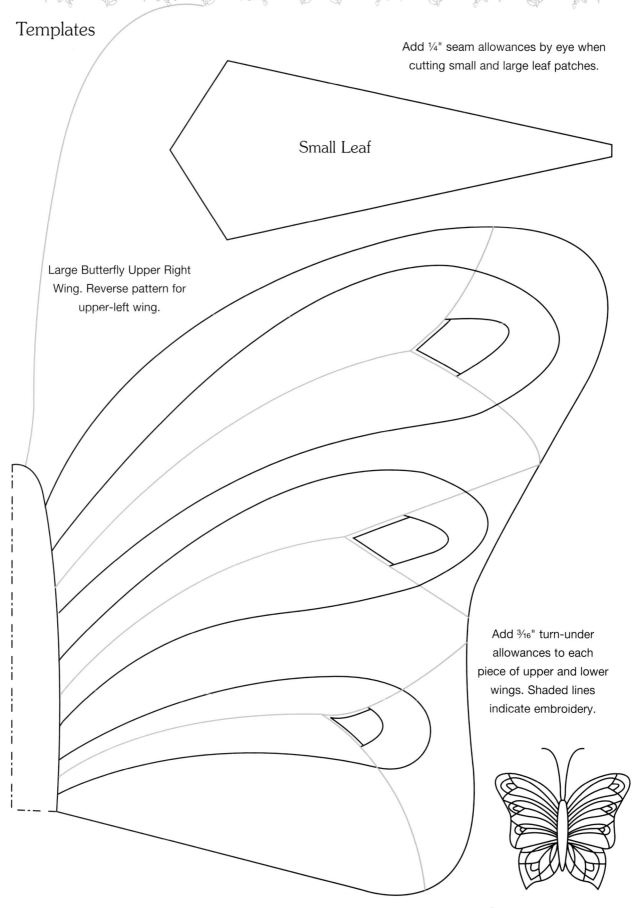

Small Leaf

Large Butterfly Upper Right Wing. Reverse pattern for upper-left wing.

Add ³⁄₁₆" turn-under allowances to each piece of upper and lower wings. Shaded lines indicate embroidery.

Templates

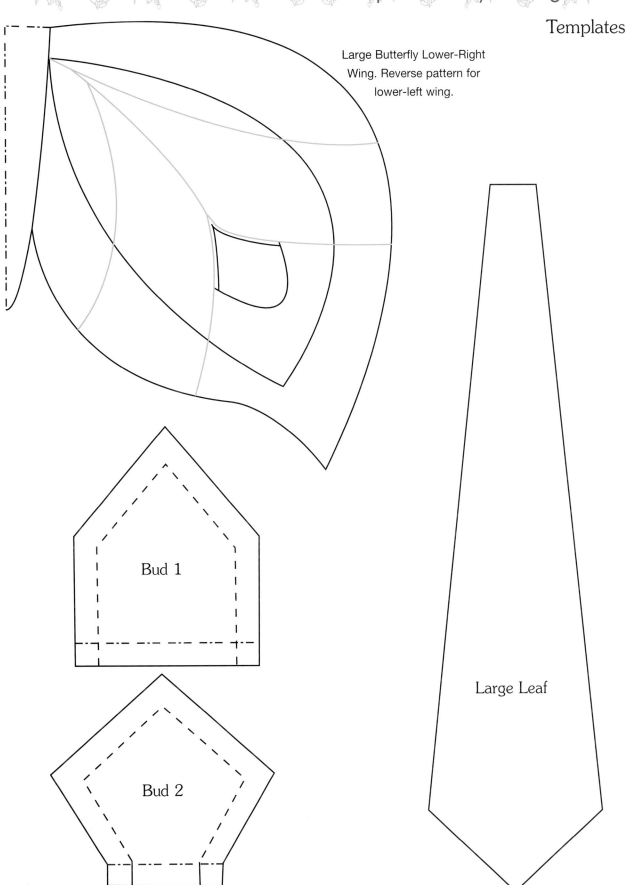

Large Butterfly Lower-Right Wing. Reverse pattern for lower-left wing.

Bud 1

Bud 2

Large Leaf

Meet Dawn Cameron-Dick

I was probably born with a needle in my hand, and even in my early years, knitting, crocheting, and embroidery were a part of my life. I also designed and sewed clothes for myself and costumes for local theater productions.

In 1971, I had my first child and decided to be a real "Earth Mother" by making him a quilt. That is where my self-teaching began. By trial and error, I spent the next few years figuring out just how these wonderful creations are constructed.

Living for seven years in Saudi Arabia in the 1970s gave me the time to develop my skills, and after returning to the United States with my new British husband, I had the courage to open a quilt shop in Colorado. I was fortunate enough to have Judith Baker Montano as a neighbor and friend, which helped my confidence grow.

Five years later, my husband's career took us to Belgium, where I was sure no one would be the least bit interested in my quilting. As it turned out, it was just the right place at the right time, because I became one of the founding members of the Belgian quilt guild and taught quiltmaking nearly every working day of the eight years we spent there. In 1996, we decided to settle in the south of England, where I now lecture and teach full time.

Designing TRY TO REMEMBER

The quilt is designed in a very traditional style, but I wanted to use some modern techniques to make it. So, half the quilt is stitched by hand and half with invisible machine appliqué. I believe it is nearly impossible to tell which is which – an opinion shared by the judges who wanted to award it first place in hand appliqué because they couldn't believe the machine was involved. All the quilting is by hand, and the gently curved lines reflect the flowing lines of the appliqué.

I love autumn colors and am fascinated by four-block quilts. The urns in the border are the large stone urns in my garden, and the corner trees represent the apple and pear trees in my orchard. The quilt would be striking in forest green and burgundy or rose pink and soft, spring green.

I wanted an airy, lacy feeling to the quilt and wanted the design to be one that most appliquérs could do. I hope you will give it a try and have as much pleasure in making it as I did.

TRY TO REMEMBER, 74" x 74", made by Dawn Cameron-Dick

Try to Remember
Pattern

This beauty will provide many relaxing hours of hand or machine work. Take time to savor re-creating this classic design or use the appliqué motifs to create your own wallhanging or bed quilt.

To simplify this project, smooth the outline of the oak leaves by eliminating all the little projections. Replace the trees and Flower-3 with more of Flowers-1 and 2. Substitute a 2" (finished 1½") round circle for the yo-yos in Flower-2. You can also replace the pots and urns with some simplified oak leaves or more flowers, buds, or leaves.

Buying and Cutting

Fabrics	Yds.	No. of Pieces
White	6	4 squares 25½"
borders		4 strips 13½" x 76½"
binding		8 strips 2½" x 42"
Medium rust	¾	48 C, pieced flower
		20 flower-2
		20 yo-yos
		(3½" circles)
Dark rust	2	4 A, 48 D,
		pieced flower
		4 tree pots
		32 rose buds
		(6½" circles)
		24 flower-1
		12 apples
Gold	½	16 B, pieced flower
		4 flower-3
		8 birds
		8 bird wings
		24 flower-1 centers
		(1½" circles)
Orange gold	⅛	12 pears
Green	3⅜	112 large leaves
		76 small leaves
		16 oak leaves
		32 calyxes
		4 flower-3 bases
		4 trees
bias tube		1 square 27"
Brown	¼	4 flower urns
Backing	4½	2 panels 39½" x 78"
Batting		78" x 78"

Supplies

Gold and green or brown embroidery thread for the flowers and fruit stems
Template material

Appliqué Preparation

Make plastic or lightweight cardboard templates for the appliqué patterns listed in the table. Use the templates to make the number of pieces required (Patterns begin on page 58).

Bias tubes – Make a continuous bias strip 1" wide by 16½" yards long from the 27" green square. Fold the bias strip in half, right side out. Sew the raw edges together with a ¼" seam allowance to make a tube. Trim the allowances to ⅛". Cut the tube into convenient lengths and press the seam allowances to the back so they will not show.

Rose buds – To make the three-dimensional buds, fold each 6½" dark rust circle in half, then fold both bottom corners to the center as shown in Figure 1, Steps 1 and 2. Baste with a running stitch, about a fourth of the way up from the bottom. Pull the thread to gather the fabric (Figure 1, Step 3).

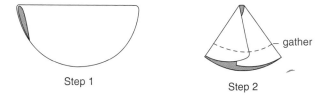

Step 1   Step 2 — gather

Step 3

Fig. 1. Fold the bottom corners, gather the circle, and stitch.

Flower-1 – This flower will be embroidered after it is appliquéd in place. See Step 4 on page 58.

Flower-2 – To make the yo-yos for the center of each flower, turn under a ¼" allowance around each 3½" medium rust circle. Sew the allowance to the circle with a running stitch (Figure 2). Pull the thread

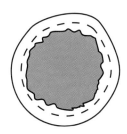

Fig. 2. Sew turn-under allowance with a running stitch.

Fig. 3. Pull thread to gather.

to gather the circle and anchor with a couple of stitches (Figure 3). Appliqué the yo-yos to the flowers.

Flower-3 – Patches C and D can be paper foundation pieced, if you like. Appliqué the B pieces to the A's. Then appliqué the A/B center to the C/D ring (pattern on page 60).

Block Construction

Refer to the quilt photo on page 55 for placing the various pieces.

1. Fold each 25½" white square in half diagonally in both directions and crease the folds.

2. Using the creases as placement guides, appliqué the bias stems to the square.

3. Add the pieced oak leaves and then the pieced flowers in the center of the blocks.

4. Appliqué the rest of flowers, buds, and leaves and embroider the flower-1 pieces. If desired, cut the background from behind the larger pieces, leaving a ⅛" allowance. Trim the blocks to 24½".

Border Construction

1. Sew the four blocks together and measure for border length.

2. The borders have a couple of inches of extra length for custom fitting. Mark the actual measurements on the border so you will know the limits for placing the appliqué. Fold the border strips in half lengthwise and crosswise. Use the creases for placing the bias strips and the motifs.

3. Appliqué the borders strips, except for the corner pieces, and sew the border strips to the quilt with mitered corners. Add the trees, birds, and pots to the corners.

Quilting Pattern

Layer and baste the quilt. A flower is quilted in the center of the quilt, and the rest of the background is quilted in waves. Patterns are on pages 59 and 60.

Finishing

Use your favorite method to bind the quilt. There are enough 2½" strips to make double-fold binding with mitered corners.

Templates

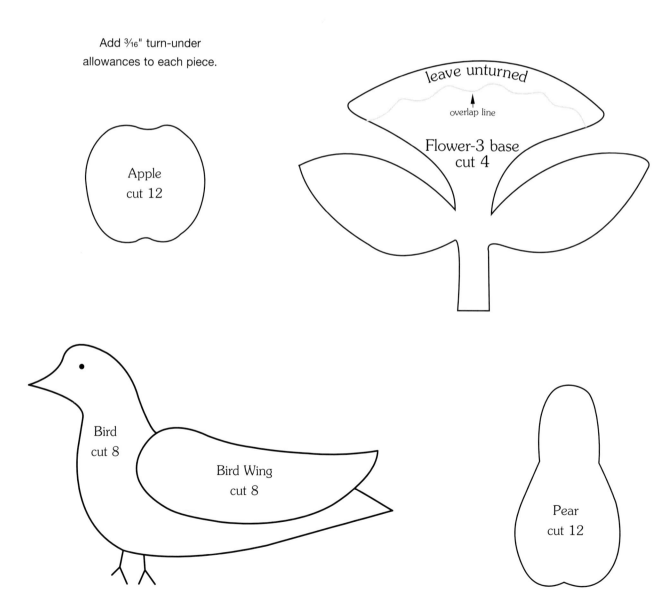

Add ³⁄₁₆" turn-under allowances to each piece.

leave unturned

overlap line

Flower-3 base
cut 4

Apple
cut 12

Bird
cut 8

Bird Wing
cut 8

Pear
cut 12

PIECED OR APPLIQUÉD FLOWERS - Dawn Cameron-Dick

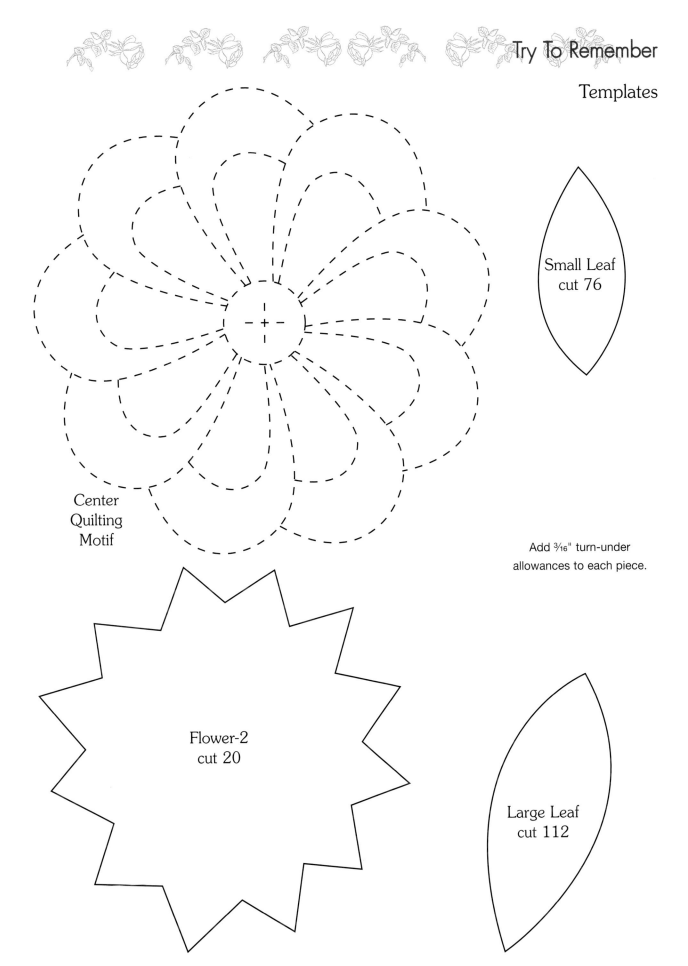

Small Leaf
cut 76

Center
Quilting
Motif

Add 3/16" turn-under
allowances to each piece.

Flower-2
cut 20

Large Leaf
cut 112

Templates

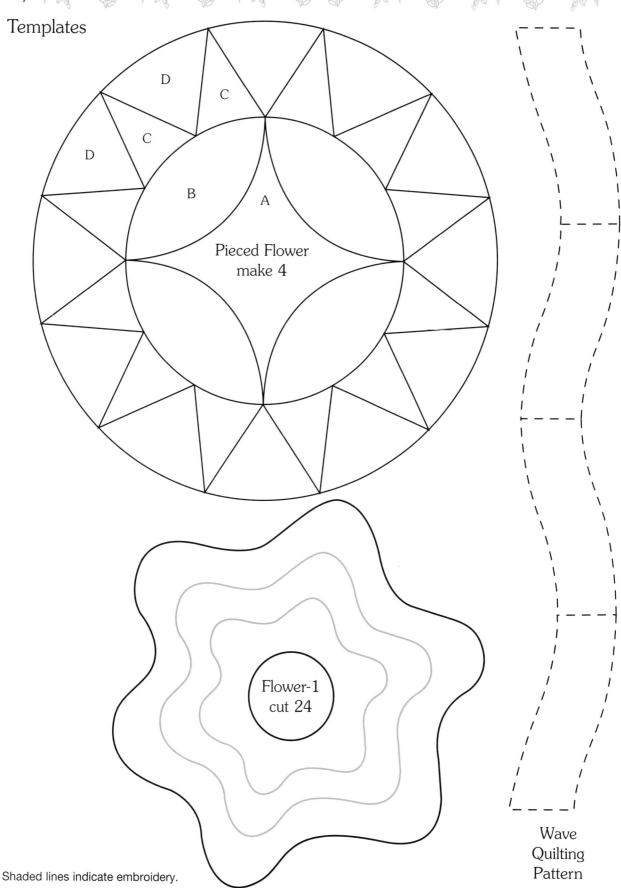

D

C

D C

D

B A

Pieced Flower
make 4

Flower-1
cut 24

Wave
Quilting
Pattern

Shaded lines indicate embroidery.

PIECED OR APPLIQUÉD FLOWERS - Dawn Cameron-Dick

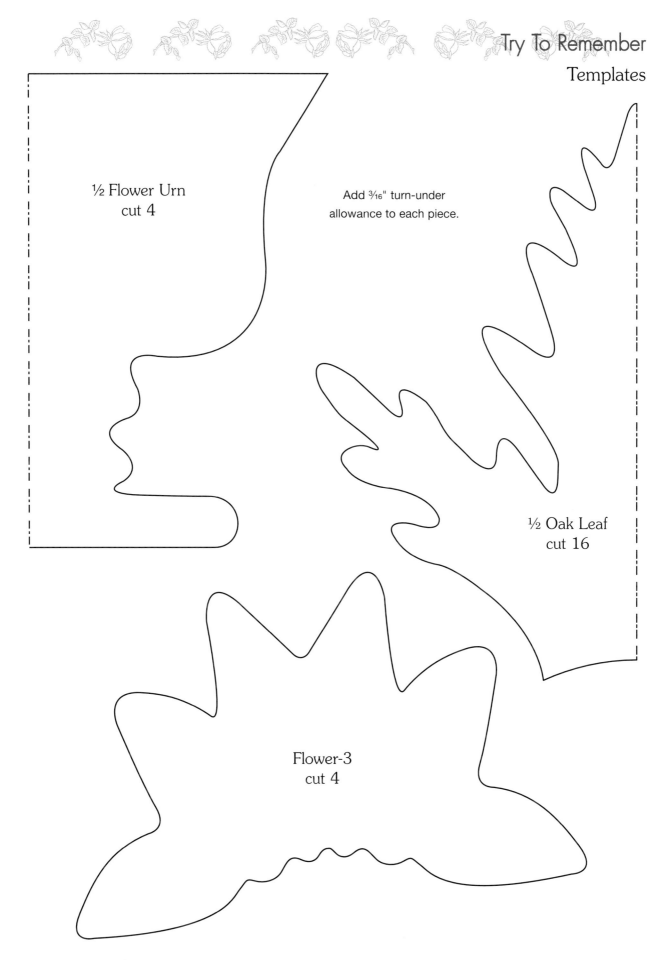

½ Flower Urn
cut 4

Add ³⁄₁₆" turn-under
allowance to each piece.

½ Oak Leaf
cut 16

Flower-3
cut 4

Templates

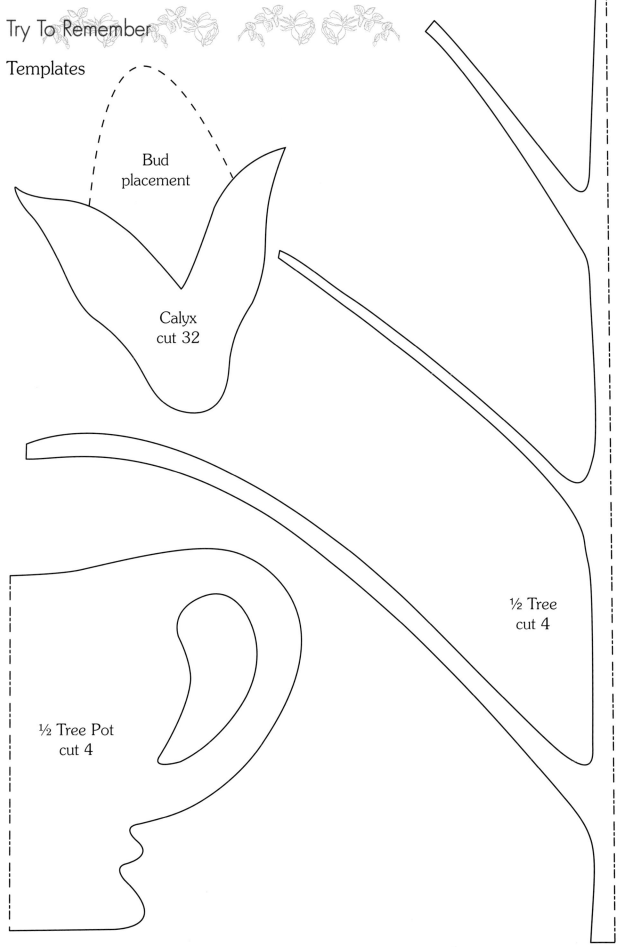

Bud
placement

Calyx
cut 32

½ Tree
cut 4

½ Tree Pot
cut 4

Add 3/16" turn-under
allowance to each piece.

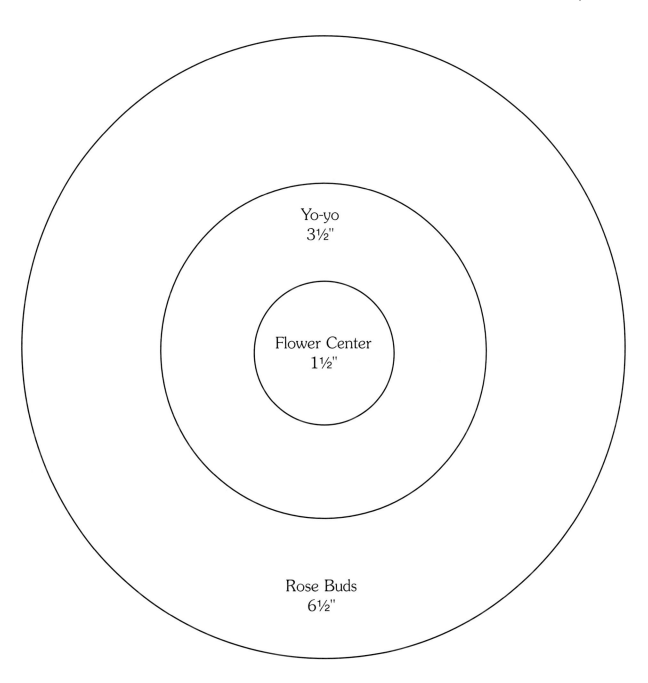

Yo-yo
3½"

Flower Center
1½"

Rose Buds
6½"

$\mathcal{M}$eet Janis Benedict

My introduction to quilting began in 1995 with a basic class at a fabric store. I was so captivated by the process that I produced three different versions of the project, and exclaimed to myself, "I can do this!" Life as I knew it had changed.

I now dream in colored fabric. Whether standing in line, waiting on hold, or traveling in the car, I'm thinking of quilt designs. Several quilt projects have even been designed under water during my exercise time in the pool.

I like working with traditional geometric designs and altering them to produce bolder, more colorful results. It is intriguing to change a pattern to create an illusion of depth, movement, or light. There seem to be sources for design inspiration everywhere in the world. Sometimes they are in nature, like a garden of daylilies moving in the summer breeze. Sometimes they are in funny places, like junk mail. One aspect of being a quilter is the constant mental stimulation of reinterpreting things I see into two-dimensional patterns, color, and fabric.

$\mathcal{D}$esigning DAYLILIES

My goal for this quilt was to create the illusion of movement and strong color that you see in a garden of daylilies. Early in my quiltmaking, I was intrigued by the article "Patterns in Motion" by Lenore Parham, (*Threads*, May 1993) in which she explained a technique for drafting an asymmetrical block to produce the perception of movement in the overall design.

The off-center Pineapple block was first drafted on the computer. New deli sandwich wrap is my favorite paper-foundation tissue because it is easy to see through and tear. I taped a sheet of sandwich wrap to a sheet of printer paper so it would feed smoothly through the printer to transfer the design onto the tissue. Each block was then paper-foundation pieced.

The flower fabric was used as the basis for color choices, with consideration given to the natural deep greens, strong yellows, and reds found in daylilies.

The border was designed as an extension of the geometric forms created by the pattern of Pineapple blocks so that the angles matched between the blocks and border. I pinned the quilt edge to a strip of tissue paper and drew the pattern for the border strip, which made it easy to paper-piece the strip.

DAYLILIES, 28" x 40", made by Janis Benedict

Daylilies
Pattern

This paper-foundation-pieced Pineapple quilt derives its energy from the asymmetry of the blocks and the bright colors. Note the contrast between the fabric pattern in the center squares and the floral strips.

To simplify this project, replace both borders with a single red border, cut 2½" wide (purchase an additional ⅜" yard). The corners can be butted or mitered.

Buying and Cutting

Fabrics	Yds.	No. of Pieces
White	⅜	3 strips 1½"
		3 strips 1"
		4 border strips 12¾" x 50½"
Yellow-1	¼	4 strips 1½"
Yellow-2	¼	4 strips 1½"
Yellow-3	⅜	10 F
		4 strips 1½"
Green	1¼	4 D, 6 F
		11 strips 1"
binding		4 strips 2½"
Floral	½	10 A
		10 strips 1½"
Red	⅝	6 B, 4 C, 4 Cr, 6 E, 6 Er, 2 G, 2 Gr, 2 H, 2 Hr
		6 strips 1"
		2 strips 1¾"
Orange	⅛	2 strips 1½"
Backing	1⅜	1 panel 28" x 44"
Batting		28" x 44"

r = reverse

Freezer-Paper Foundations
12 as shown
12 reversed

Quilt Construction

Use strips of the appropriate color and width to paper piece 12 blocks as shown and 12 blocks with the pattern reversed (pattern on page 68).

Arrange the blocks in six rows of four alternating types and rotate them as needed to create the pattern (Figure 1).

Fig. 1. Rotating the blocks creates the star pattern.

Border 1 – For each side border, use three A's and two B's. For the top and bottom borders, sew two A's and one B. Add a C on one end of each strip and a Cr on the other. Sew these borders to the quilt and add a green D patch at each corner.

Border 2 – For each side border, use two E's, two Er's, two green F's, and three yellow F's. Add an H to one end and an Hr to the other. For the top and bottom, use one E, one Er, one green F, and two yellow F's. Add a G to one end and a Gr to the other. Sew the side border strips on first, then the top and bottom (Figure 2).

Quilting Pattern

Layer the backing, batting and quilt top. Baste the layers. DAYLILIES is quilted in the ditch around the pattern pieces.

Finishing

Use your favorite method to bind the quilt. There are enough 2½" strips to make double-fold binding with mitered corners.

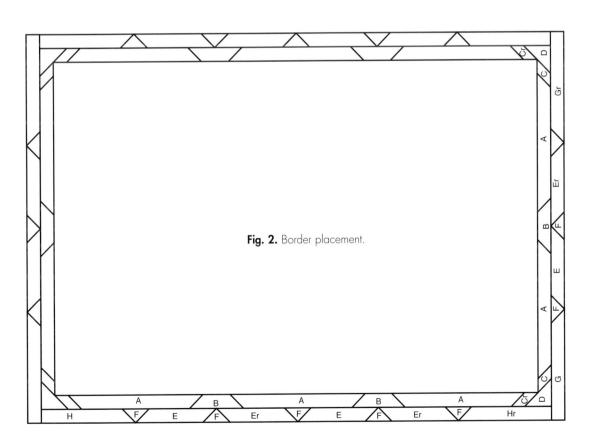

Fig. 2. Border placement.

Foundation - Piecing Templates

Template includes ¼"
seam allowances on
outside edges.

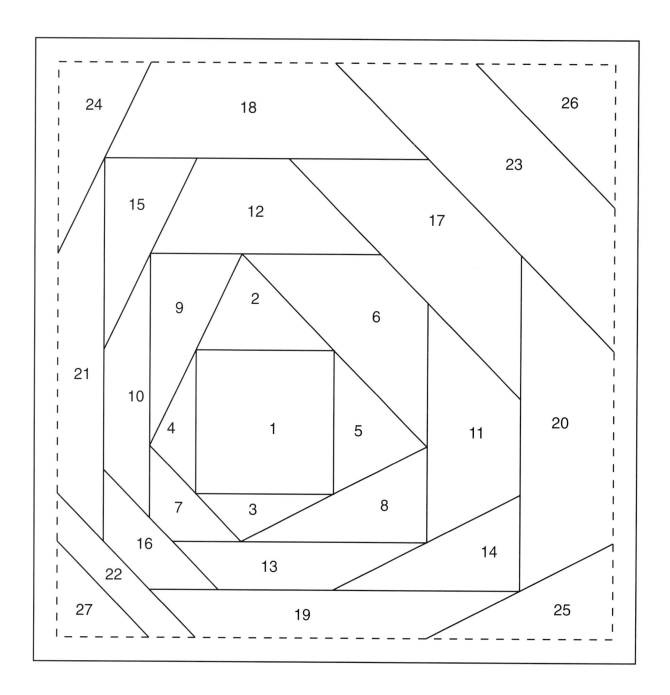

Templates

Templates include ¼" seam allowances.

r = reverse

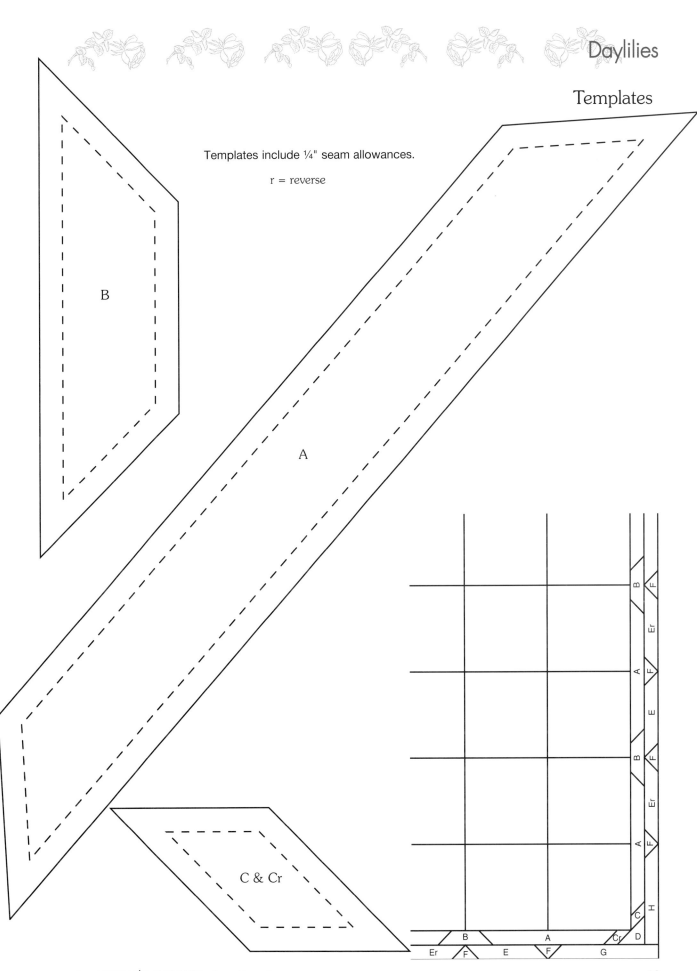

B

A

C & Cr

PIECED OR APPLIQUÉD FLOWERS - Janis Benedict

Templates

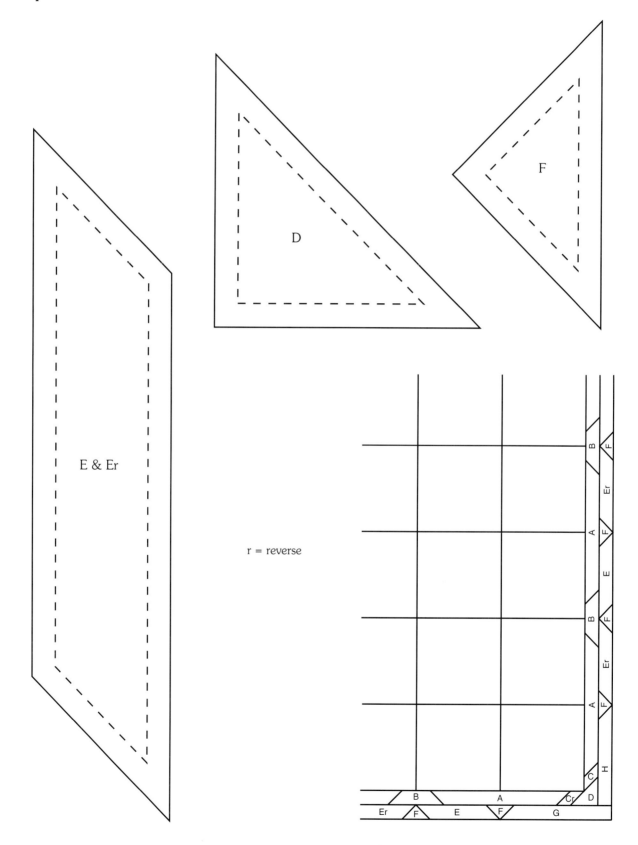

F

D

E & Er

r = reverse

B
F
Er
A
F
E
B
F
Er
A
F

C
H
B
A
Cr
D
Er
F
E
F
G

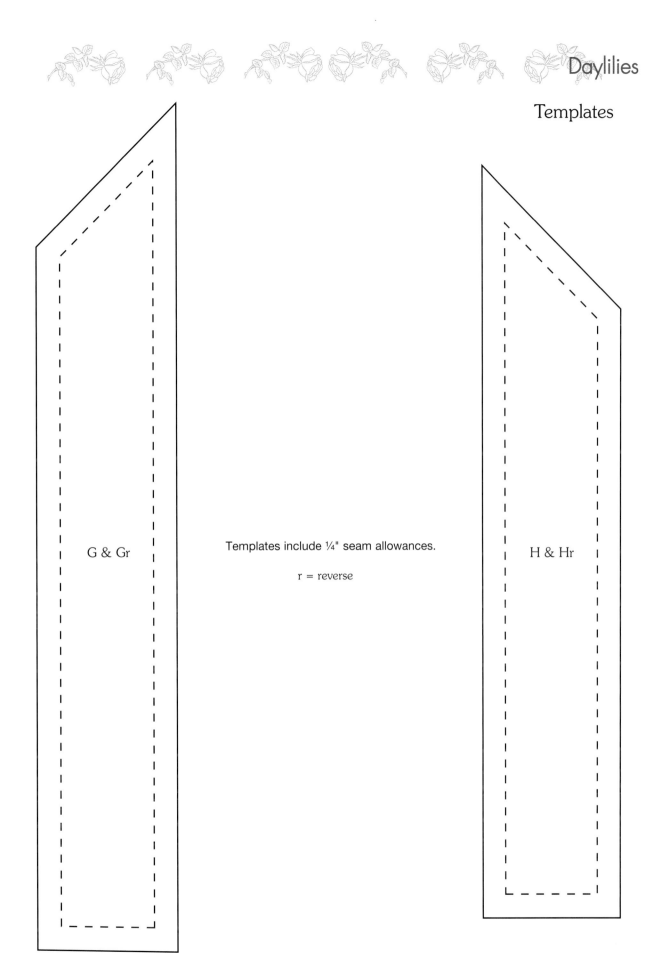

G & Gr

Templates include ¼" seam allowances.

r = reverse

H & Hr

ℳeet Chris Taricani

I made my first quilt while studying art in college in the 1970s. I had always loved the graphic and tactile qualities of antique quilts, so for an independent study project for a craft class, I knew I had to make a quilt. My professor had other ideas. He thought that crafts should be made of wood and should involve the use of power tools. I did convince him to let me make the quilt but had to agree to make something with wood as well. I have never done any type of woodworking again, but I was hooked on quiltmaking.

I usually take a rather haphazard approach to designing my quilts. I like to start with a traditional block. My favorites are circular patterns like Mariner's Compass, and I never know what the finished quilt will look like until it is actually done. At any one time, I am working on three or four quilts that are in various stages of completion.

I always use many fabrics in each quilt, mainly to experiment with the way different fabrics work together. Using different fabrics in each block also prevents me from getting bored while sewing. From the creative energy of designing and piecing to the soothing rhythm of hand quilting, I love every step involved in the making of a quilt. I intend to be quilting for a long time to come and have the fabric stash to prove it!

𝒟esigning HOFFMAN HYBRID LILY

I chose the New York Beauty block for this quilt and hand-pieced a few of the blocks but didn't know what to do with them. The blocks began to look like flowers, and three of them put together reminded me of the traditional Carolina Lily pattern. At this point, I decided to add the appliquéd stems and leaves.

For some inexplicable reason, I am drawn to fabrics with sun faces and buy as many as possible. You just never know when the manufacturers are going to stop making them. I try to sneak a few sun faces into most of my quilts – in this case as the sashing cornerstones. They add a touch of whimsy to the quilt. I then added the flying geese border, opting for a subtle coloration that complemented the center of the quilt better than the higher-contrast border originally planned. The hand quilting is done freehand because, if I were to name my least favorite part of quiltmaking, it would be marking the quilting lines. The sashing and binding are striped fabrics, just because I really love stripes.

HOFFMAN HYBRID LILY, 30" x 30", made by Chris Taricani

Hoffman Hybrid Lily
Pattern

HOFFMAN HYBRID LILY **was originally made for the 1997 Hoffman Challenge,** where it won honorable mention in the mixed-technique category. Notice that, while scraps are used for the lilies, the blocks are unified by the use of a single fabric in the B patches in all the flowers.

To simplify this project, replace the flying-geese border with a plain border, or replace just the flying-geese sections, keeping the square-within-a-square center and corner pieces.

Buying and Cutting

Fabrics	Yds.	No. of Pieces
*Scraps	½	12 A, 12 B, 60 C, 48 D, 12 E, 12 Er, 4 K, 8 M, 8 Q, 12 R, 9 S
*Cream	1½	12 F, 8 G, 4-6½"squares, 144 J
Green	⅝	8 N, 8 P
bias tube (stems)		1 square 18"
*Beige	⅜	56 L, 4 K
Striped sashing	¼	12 strips 1½" x 11"
Backing	1	1 panel 34" x 34"
Binding	⅜	4 strips 2½"
Batting		34" x 34"

r = reverse

*See Construction Alternatives on page 75. The methods you choose will determine how some of the patches are cut.

Construction Alternatives

There are several methods you can use to construct the lily blocks and border. Choose the ones you like from the following descriptions:

• Use paper foundations to make the arcs for the lilies (patches C, D, E, and Er) or cut individual patches for piecing.

• Use curved piecing to sew patches A, B, and the arc or appliqué the three pieces together.

• Cut the background patch (F) for the lily as a 5¼" square and appliqué the completed lily to the patch. Trim the background away from under the lily, leaving a ¼" seam allowance. Or, cut F as a curved piece and use curved piecing to sew the completed lily to F.

• Cut J, K, and L as separate patches and sew together, or use the following rotary-cutting technique. Cut patches J = 2" square, K = 3½" square, L = 2" x 3½" rectangle. Place a J square in the corner of a K square or L rectangle. Draw a diagonal line across the J square and sew on the line. Trim off the extra fabric in the corner, leaving a ¼" seam allowance. Repeat for all the J patches.

Quilt Construction

1. Choose the methods you would like to use for making the lily blocks, center squares, corner squares, and Flying Geese.

2. Make any templates or foundations needed. Cut the number of pieces listed in the Buying and Cutting table. Make 12 lily blocks.

3. Make 1 yard of green bias tubing from the 18" green square, as follows: Cut continuous bias 1" wide. Fold strips in half, right side out. Sew tubes with a ¼" seam allowance. Trim allowances to ⅛". Press the seam to the back so it will not show.

4. Appliqué the bias stems and leaf pieces M, N, P, and Q to the 6½" cream squares. There's no need to turn under the raw bias ends of the stems at the edges of the block because they will be sewn into the seams. Trim the squares to 6¼".

5. Sew three lily blocks together with one appliquéd square and two G patches to make a four-block unit. Make four of these units. Appliqué an R patch at the base of each flower.

6. Sew two sashing strips together with three setting squares (S) to make a sashing row, as shown in Figure 1. Make three sashing rows.

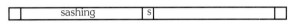

Fig. 1. *Sashing row; make three.*

7. Sew two four-block units and three sashing strips together to make a block row (Figure 2). Make two block rows. Sew the sashing rows and block rows together as shown on page 76.

Fig. 2. *Block row; make two.*

Border Construction

Using the templates, cut 56 flying geese, four corner squares, and four center squares, or you can use the corner-square method, described below, to make these units.

Corner squares – There is enough fabric in the yardage calculations to use the corner-square method for making the flying geese, corner squares, and center squares. There is some wasted fabric with this method, but the increased speed and accuracy can be worth it.

Instead of cutting triangles for the J patches, rotary cut 2" squares. For the L patches, cut 2" x 3½" rectangles, and for K, cut 3½" squares.

Place a J square on one end of an L rectangle and draw a diagonal line on the square.

Sew on the line and cut off the extra triangles, leaving a ¼" seam allowance (Figure 3). Repeat on the other side of the rectangle to complete the flying geese unit (Figure 4). If you like, you can sew the extra triangles together, either before or after you cut them off, and save them for another project.

Use this same method to add the J triangles to the K squares for the center and corner pieces.

To make a border unit, sew seven flying geese units together, with the geese all pointing in the same direction. Make eight border units.

Sew a center square between two border units, with the flying geese pointing toward the square. Make four border strips like this. Sew a strip to the right and left sides of the quilt. Add a corner square to each end of the two remaining strips and sew them to the top and bottom of the quilt.

Quilting Pattern

The flower petals (C patches) have been quilted in the ditch. Echo quilting has been used in the G and E patches, and the flying geese, center squares, and corner squares have been outline quilted.

Finishing

Use your favorite method to bind the quilt. There are enough 2½" strips to make double-fold binding with mitered corners.

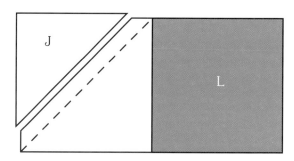

Fig. 3. Draw diagonal line, stitch, and trim away corners.

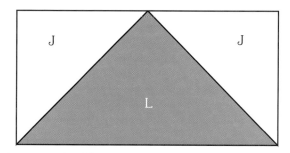

Fig. 4. Completed flying geese unit.

Quilt Assembly Diagram

PIECED OR APPLIQUÉD FLOWERS - Chris Taricani

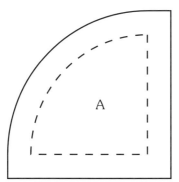

A

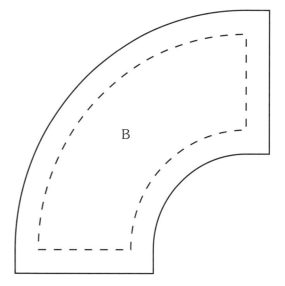

B

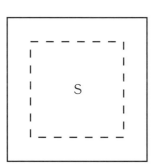

S

Templates include ¼" seam allowances.

r = reverse

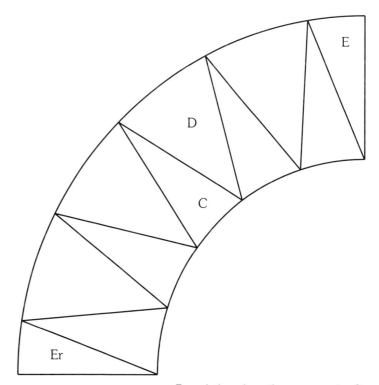

E

D

C

Er

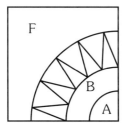

F

B

A

Lily block

Foundation piece the arc or make C,
D, and E/Er templates to cut patches
individually. Be sure to add ¼" seam
allowances to fabric patches.

Templates

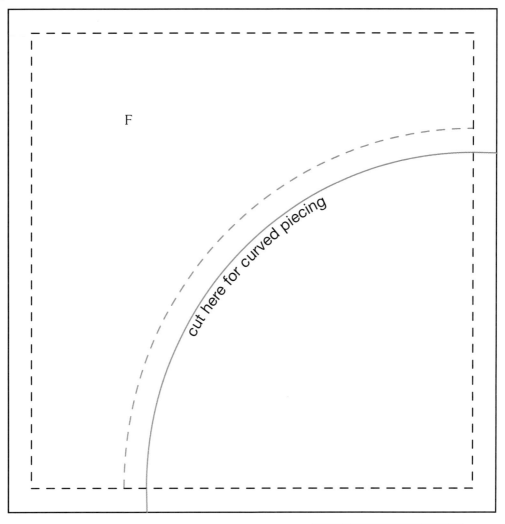

F

cut here for curved piecing

Four-block unit

Templates include ¼" seam allowances.

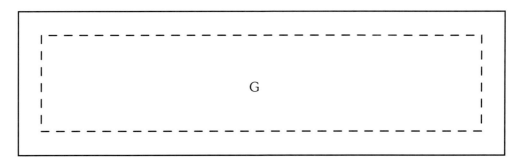

G

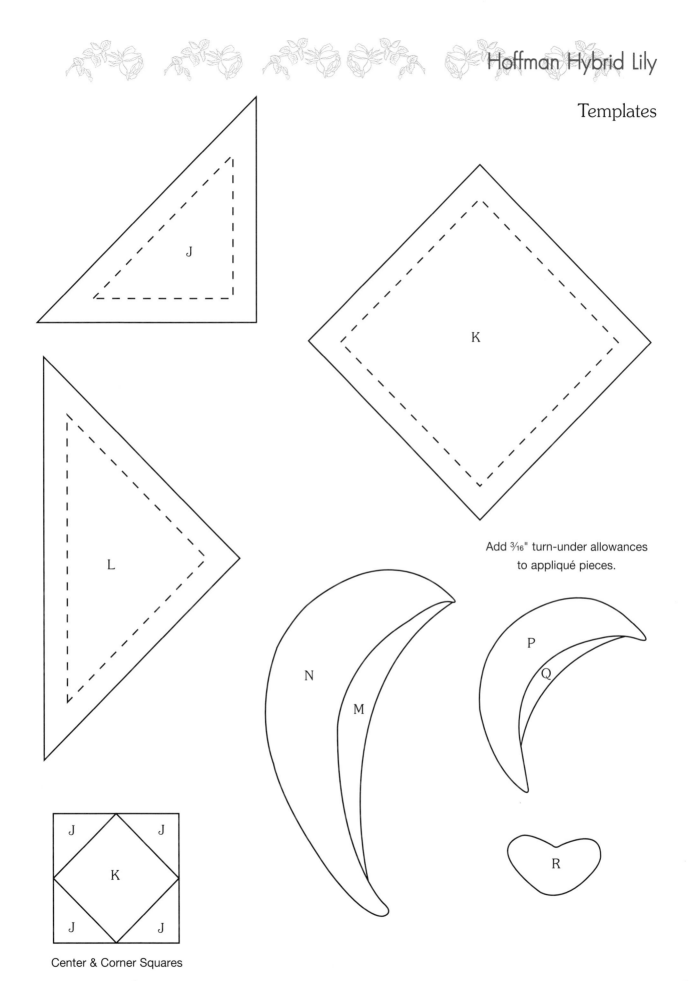

J

K

L

Add ³⁄₁₆" turn-under allowances
to appliqué pieces.

N

M

P
Q

R

J   J

K

J   J

Center & Corner Squares

PIECED OR APPLIQUÉD FLOWERS - Chris Taricani

This is only a small selection of the books available from the American Quilter's Society. AQS books are known worldwide for timely topics, clear writing, beautiful color photos, and accurate illustrations and patterns. These books are available from your local bookseller, quilt shop or public library.

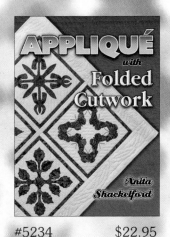

#5234 $22.95

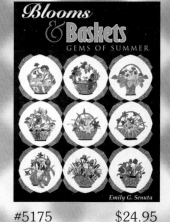

#5175 $24.95

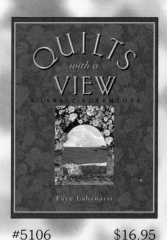

#5106 $16.95

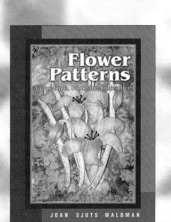

#5238 $19.95

#4833 $14.95

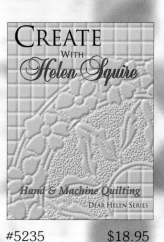

#5235 $18.95

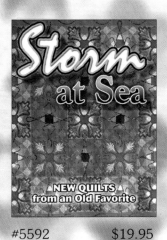

#5592 $19.95

#5296 $16.95

#4911 $16.95

Look for these books nationally or call
1-800-626-5420